The

SOUTHERN
KETO

Cookbook

The
SOUTHERN
KETO

Cookbook

---

100 HIGH-FAT, LOW-CARB RECIPES FOR CLASSIC COMFORT FOOD

Emilie Bailey

Photography by Laura Flippen

ROCKRIDGE
PRESS

For general information on our other products and services or to obtain technical support, please contact our Customer Care Department within the United States at (866) 744-2665, or outside the United States at (510) 253-0500.

Rockridge Press publishes its books in a variety of electronic and print formats. Some content that appears in print may not be available in electronic books, and vice versa.

TRADEMARKS: Rockridge Press and the Rockridge Press logo are trademarks or registered trademarks of Callisto Media Inc. and/or its affiliates, in the United States and other countries, and may not be used without written permission. All other trademarks are the property of their respective owners. Rockridge Press is not associated with any product or vendor mentioned in this book.

Interior and Cover Designer: Julie Schrader
Art Producer: Sara Feinstein
Editor: Rebecca Markley
Production Editor: Emily Sheehan
Photography © 2020 Laura Flippen.
Author photo courtesy of © Melissa Regeon Photography.

ISBN: Print 978-1-64611-551-8 | eBook 978-1-64611-552-5
R0

*To my Cowboy and my girls, Maddie and Paige . . .
you inspire me more than you'll ever know.*

CONTENTS

INTRODUCTION

I'll never forget Christmas morning when I was six, walking into my living room and seeing the brand-new, gorgeous pink Barbie kitchen Santa had left for me. This was when it all started: The stars aligned and this was the moment in my life when I knew cooking and food were my passions. To give credit where credit is due, my love of cooking really took root long before that, in the kitchens of the most influential women in my life—my Nana, Big Granny, Granny, my great aunts, and my Moms, Sandy and Laurie. These kitchens were full of the aromas of incredible, home-cooked food, echoing with the sounds of laughter and chaos, and filled with an overwhelming sense of joy and togetherness. This is where I grew up, and from the floors of these busy kitchens, I learned the importance of food, family, and tradition.

I'm a seventh-generation Texas girl, a mom, wife, former restaurateur, and outdoor enthusiast with a deep love and affection for the home-cooked Texas and Southern comfort foods I grew up eating. Biscuits and gravy, fried pork chops with rice and gravy (oh, how I love gravy!), dumplings, buttermilk pie, fresh whipped cream . . . oh, lord, I could go on and on. That being said, over the past 20 years, I have learned that incredible, stick-to-your ribs, comfort food doesn't have to be filled with sugar, grains, and starches, and with a few creative tweaks and an open mind, it's possible to enjoy all these delicious foods and more, while maintaining a keto lifestyle.

Like many people, I've struggled with my weight since my late teens. Aggravated by medical conditions beyond my control, or so I thought, I surrendered to the fact that I was just meant to struggle. It wasn't until my oldest daughter began to experience issues with her health that I realized it was time to make a permanent change for both of us.

These days, I live on a ranch out in the middle of Texas with my husband, the Cowboy; and my two girls, Maddie and Paige; where we raise animals and I cook for hungry ranch guests. Out here, snake boots are typical footwear. We talk to our chickens. Most days we have no concept of time. Our welcome mat is always covered with hay—and you may find us with a little in our hair on occasion. We make new traditions. Family dinners are a priority. Most nights our kitchen is loud and full of laughter. Biscuits and gravy are still king, but now they're ketofied. My recipes are inspired by the traditional comfort foods I grew up enjoying, with a modern keto twist, and are always kid- and Cowboy-approved.

So grab a seat and make yourself at home. I've got some new recipes that will flip the lid on your idea of what keto food can be, and I promise not all things deliciously Southern are chicken-fried and served up with a side of gravy!

1

THE SOUTHERN KETO KITCHEN

Hold your horses! Before we jump right into the kitchen, we need to do a little housekeeping. In this chapter, we're going to run through the basics of keto, like why your macros are important, what foods to enjoy and what to avoid, and ingredients to keep on hand in your keto kitchen. You may be surprised that Southern comfort food can be keto but, in fact, Southern cuisine and keto are two peas in a pod.

Today's Southern Cuisine and Keto

When someone mentions Southern food, what's the first image your mind conjures up? A gorgeous mound of golden fried chicken or maybe a pot of braised greens with salt pork? How 'bout a basket of steaming-hot, fluffy buttermilk biscuits, a skillet of spicy shrimp jambalaya, or a pan of cobbler studded with juicy seasonal fruit? If any of these scrumptious images came to mind, you'd be right. They're all Southern dishes.

Today's Southern cuisine cannot be defined by any one state, dish, or specific cooking method; it's a cuisine just as diverse as the people, families, places, and pasts it comes from. Recipes and techniques have been passed down through generations, along with a deep love, respect, and pride in the traditions and heritage of their kin-folks. These regional traditions, along with the friendly, community-centered culture of the South, otherwise known as "Southern hospitality," permeate deeply into the regional food and ignite the overwhelming feeling that you are home.

Southern cuisine is something you experience. It tells a story, evokes emotions, allows us to relive special moments past, reconnect with our loved ones through familiar tastes and aromas, and brings people and communities together—family, neighbors, friends, even strangers. Often created by necessity, these rustic dishes focused on the resources available and plentiful to people in the region where they lived. When it came down to it, many times, folks just had to make do with what they had, and make the best out of it, to feed their families.

Southern food is steeped in rich history and culture, but also has quite a bit in common with "modern" food trends. "Farm to table," "clean eating," "nose to tail,"— Southern cooks were on the forefront of these food trends. In a traditional Southern kitchen, you'd find simple, unassuming dishes like burgoo, fried catfish, or braised greens, cooked with love and prepared with fresh, unprocessed, seasonal ingredients. These ingredients were sometimes in short supply, so cooks would go to painstaking lengths to preserve them: canning, curing, drying, and repurposing what they could to ensure as little waste as possible.

At first glance, today's Southern cuisine and the keto lifestyle are completely incompatible, but once you dig a little deeper, you see they're truly cut from the same cloth. Fresh vegetables, full-fat dairy, unprocessed meats, eggs, and unrefined fats like butter, lard, and tallow are staples of a traditional Southern kitchen . . . and the keto diet. Now, of course, that doesn't mean all Southern dishes are keto friendly, but it does give us some common ground to adapt Southern comfort food classics into keto recipes that I guarantee will be slap yo' momma good!

Keto Basics

Keto, or the ketogenic diet, is a high-fat, moderate-protein, and very-low-carbohydrate way of eating that, when done properly, can offer incredible health benefits including weight loss, improved blood glucose, decreased inflammation, improvement in other health markers, increased energy and mental clarity, and so much more. Originally formulated back in the early 20th century by doctors as a treatment for people who suffered from epilepsy, today the ketogenic diet is back on the dietary scene, challenging our old, outdated beliefs about what "healthy" food is.

Within the realm of the keto lifestyle, there are a few variations of the diet you've probably heard about (dirty, lazy, etc.), but a proper keto diet focuses on eliminating foods that cause blood sugar and insulin levels to rise or spike, so your body can achieve a state of ketosis where it's using fat for fuel instead of glucose. In other words, the ketogenic diet focuses on removing foods from our diet that our body converts into sugar or glucose. In general, restricting carbohydrates forces the body to burn fat—both dietary and bodily fats—as fuel in the form of ketones instead of using glucose for its primary fuel source. I've always joked I wish my body would just "eat itself." Well, in a state of ketosis, it practically does!

So, you're ready to go whole hog on the keto lifestyle and get your body into ketosis and burning fat. How exactly do you do that? Here are the keto principles you need so you can get started in two shakes of a lamb's tail.

MACRONUTRIENTS

You will hear the word "macros" thrown around quite a bit in keto circles. The word "macros" is simply short for "macronutrients" and refers to the nutrient components—*protein*, *fat*, and *carbohydrates*—present in the foods we eat.

- PROTEINS are composed of amino acids, which are the building blocks essential for building and repairing your muscles and tissues. Getting an adequate amount of protein is critical and will vary widely based on your activity level, gender, build, age, and goals.

- FAT, in the ketogenic lifestyle, is more used as a "lever" to control hunger and help ketoers feel satiated. Note that you do not have to meet your exact fat macro. As your body becomes accustomed to using fat for fuel, your need for dietary fat will decrease. Any additional fat needed for energy will come from the fat stored in your body.

- **CARBOHYDRATES** need to be restricted for the body to enter into ketosis. To begin with, you should aim to limit your carbohydrates to 20 grams or less per day. Some people can achieve and maintain a level of ketosis with a carbohydrate intake higher than 20 grams, sometimes up to 50 grams, depending on their activity level and unique metabolism.

Most people find it beneficial to have macro guidelines when following a keto diet to help ensure the body enters a state of ketosis while still getting all the nutrition needed to thrive. Macros are typically shown as percentages of your daily calories.

FINDING YOUR PERSONAL MACROS

This is important: Your macros are a guideline and are not set in stone. You may have to tweak a few things down the road to get the results you want, so allow a little wiggle room. There are several macro calculators available online and chances are, if you try five calculators, you will get five different results. This isn't because one is more correct than the others, but rather because there really is no absolute method for macro calculation. They are unique and personal to you.

In general, a proper ketogenic diet will have the following breakdown:

- **20 PERCENT TO 25 PERCENT OF CALORIES FROM PROTEIN SOURCES** (about 0.75 grams of protein per pound of lean body mass)

- **70 PERCENT TO 75 PERCENT OF CALORIES FROM FAT** (fat intake will vary from day to day, in a range from 1 to 2 times your protein macro)

- **ABOUT 5 PERCENT OF CALORIES FROM CARBOHYDRATE SOURCES** (20 grams or fewer)

TRACKING YOUR FOOD AND MACROS

In the beginning of your keto journey, tracking what you eat and your daily macros creates a valuable guide to help make educated adjustments to your diet later if you're not getting the results you expected. Tracking your food will also help you get a handle on portion sizes. We're so used to supersize portions that we often underestimate actual portion sizes. Accurate portion sizes help ensure you're eating enough protein while staying under your carb limit, especially when you're getting started, and can save you from frustration weeks or months into your journey.

While we're on the subject of tracking, you should also monitor and track your ketone levels to make sure your hard work is paying off and you're actually in ketosis. I use a blood ketone meter, but breath meters are available as well. Beware of ketone strips—they are inexpensive but can be inaccurate.

AVOID THE "KETO FLU"

As your body switches from sugar burning to fat burning, you will more than likely notice you're shedding quite a bit of water, evidenced by multiple trips to the bathroom. This is a good thing but it can cause an imbalance in electrolytes that can cause headaches, dizziness, fatigue, etc., otherwise known as the "keto flu." Keep on top of your electrolytes from the start of your keto journey. Sodium, potassium, and magnesium are just as important to track as your macros!

So, now that you have your macros calculated and your electrolytes are in check, you're prepared to track. Now what exactly can you eat?

What to Eat and What to Cut

When enjoying the ketogenic way of eating, you will eat real, unprocessed foods—meats, veggies, full-fat dairy, healthy fats, nuts, and even some fruit on occasion. Of course, grass-fed meats and organic vegetables are great if you have access to and can afford them; if not, purchase the best quality meat and veggies you can comfortably afford. This way of life should be accessible and sustainable for everyone and doesn't have to be expensive.

ENJOY

- **BERRIES AND LOW-SUGAR FRUIT:** Measure and track berries for an accurate carb count; they are easy to underestimate.
- **FULL-FAT DAIRY:** butter, cheese, cream cheese, heavy cream, sour cream; avoid buttermilk, evaporated milk, whole milk, and yogurt due to higher carb content.
- **HEALTHY FATS:** avocado oil, butter, coconut oil, duck fat, ghee, lard, MCT, olive oil, tallow
- **HERBS AND SPICES**
- **MEAT AND POULTRY**
- **NON-STARCHY VEGETABLES:** Leafy greens like collards, kale, lettuce, spinach, and other veggies (asparagus, broccoli, Brussels sprouts, cabbage, cauliflower, celery, okra, and sauerkraut) are where your carbohydrates will come from. Some root vegetables, such as garlic, onion, radishes, squash, and turnips, can be eaten in moderation.

- **NUTS AND SEEDS:** This category also includes almond and other nut flours and butters. Avoid higher-carb nuts such as cashews and pistachios.

LIMIT

- **ALCOHOL:** Alcohol consumption will halt the fat-burning process. Enjoy the occasional glass of dry wine and stick to low-carb liquors.
- **KETO BAKED GOODS AND SWEETENERS:** Enjoy on occasion; sweeteners, even though they are keto friendly, can trigger cravings for carb-laden foods and can be easily overeaten.

AVOID

- **ALL GRAINS, STARCHES, AND LEGUMES INCLUDING SOY**
- **ARTIFICIAL SWEETENERS**
- **HIGH-CARB FRUITS AND VEGETABLES**
- **SUGAR-LADEN FOODS AND BEVERAGES**
- **UNHEALTHY VEGETABLE AND SEED OILS:** Canola seed, sunflower, and vegetable oils as well as margarine and vegetable shortening cause inflammation.

Try to avoid prepackaged food and, if it says "keto" on the packaging, chances are it's not. Always read labels—you'd be surprised where sugars and questionable ingredients are hiding. It's helpful to stick to the perimeter of the grocery store, the dairy section, produce area, and meat counter. This is the promised land of keto foods and keeps your eyes away from all the nonsense on the grocery store shelves. Even better, this is where you will find all the makings of your favorite Southern comfort food dishes.

Pantry and Refrigerator/Freezer Staples

With a fully stocked keto-friendly pantry and refrigerator, it's easy to whip up a good ol' batch of keto Southern comfort, instead of being tempted by take-out or drive-thru comfort. Here's a guide to keep you on track and keto stocked.

IN THE PANTRY

- **AVOCADO OIL:** can be heated for cooking; its mild flavor goes undetected in both savory and sweet recipes.
- **BONE BROTH (BOXED):** Buy bone broth with no added sweeteners and that is, preferably, gluten-free.
- **FLOUR:** almond and coconut, good for both baked goods and savory recipes
- **PORK RINDS OR PORK SKINS:** Even if you're not a huge fan of pork skins as a snack, they're extremely versatile in a keto kitchen and can be used as a breading, or even sweetened as a breakfast treat.
- **SWEETENERS:** Lakanto (monk fruit/erythritol blend) and HighKey (sweetener blend with allulose) brands
- **TOMATOES/TOMATO PASTE:** great for adding richness and tomato flavor to keto dishes; look for a brand with no added sugar. I like to buy tomato paste in a tube for easy storage and minimal waste.

IN THE REFRIGERATOR/FREEZER

- **ALMOND MILK (UNSWEETENED):** a dairy-free milk alternative having no sugar and very low carbs; purchase shelf-stable tetra packs, or in the dairy section of the grocery; use original (unsweetened and unflavored) for savory cooking.
- **AVOCADOS:** a great source of fat and fiber with more potassium than bananas
- **EGGS**
- **HEAVY (WHIPPING) CREAM**
- **KETO-FRIENDLY MAYONNAISE (STORE-BOUGHT OR HOMEMADE):** Great for dipping, making dips, roll ups, or mixing with hard-boiled eggs and tuna for a quick lunch.
- **BUTTER, SALTED:** Can you imagine a Southern kitchen without butter? In my recipes, I use **SALTED** butter unless otherwise noted.
- **CAULIFLOWER RICE, FROZEN:** A keto kitchen shortcut that can help get dinner on the table in a New York minute! Its mild flavor and rice-like texture make it perfect for adding to soups and casseroles, seasoning up for a side, or using as a stuffing.

SWEETENERS

Using keto-friendly sweeteners can be tricky because each has its own benefits and drawbacks, and while some of them taste similar to sugar, these sweeteners often don't act like sugar. Because we are focused on using natural ingredients, it makes sense that the sweeteners we use are naturally derived as well. Here are the most common sweeteners used in keto cooking and baking:

Allulose: Allulose is considered a rare sugar and is fairly new to the keto scene. It has no impact on blood sugar and is zero calorie since it is not digestible. It acts, bakes, and tastes like sugar since it actually is a type of sugar, but in its pure form, it's known to cause gastric distress for some and can be expensive.

Erythritol: Erythritol is a sugar alcohol found naturally in some foods that is calorie-free and does not impact blood sugar. Pure erythritol can be found in granulated and powdered forms, and is not quite as sweet as sugar. It tends to have a cooling effect when used in high concentrations, which can be off-putting, and it's sometimes blended with other sweeteners, like monk fruit or stevia, to help eliminate this aftertaste. This sweetener does not dissolve or caramelize like sugar and can cause grittiness in baked goods due to crystallization.

Monk fruit: Monk fruit is extracted from the Chinese *luo han guo* fruit and has been used for thousands of years. It has no impact on blood sugar and is similar to stevia in that it is hundreds of times sweeter than sugar, but it has no bitter aftertaste. Monk fruit extract can be found in both liquid and powdered forms, often blended with another sweetener, like erythritol, to bulk it up for baking.

Stevia: Stevia can be found in both liquid and powdered forms, has no impact on blood sugar, no caloric value, and is hundreds of times sweeter than sugar. Due to its potency and bitter aftertaste, it's often combined with other sweeteners. Beware of stevia products containing maltodextrin or dextrose. These both have a similar or higher glycemic index than actual table sugar and will spike your blood sugar.

Xylitol: Xylitol is another sugar alcohol found naturally in fruits and other foods but, unlike erythritol, it does have some impact on blood sugar and is not calorie-free. Xylitol acts and tastes more like sugar but can knock people out of ketosis due to its impact on blood sugar. It should be noted that **xylitol is deadly to dogs**, so it's a sweetener I do not use often.

After trying a mess of keto-friendly sweeteners, I've found I tend to keep two sweeteners on hand for recipes:

- A monk fruit/erythritol blend, like Lakanto brand. Lakanto makes a golden and white granulated sweetener that can be used cup for cup for sugar and also a powdered blend that's perfect to use in place of powdered sugar, that's twice as sweet as sugar. Lakanto also has liquid monk fruit extract drops for sweetening drinks, like sweet tea or smoothies, where the graininess of the erythritol may be an issue.

- A blend of allulose, monk fruit, stevia, and erythritol made by High-Key. The combination of these sweeteners plays on the strengths of each and makes it ideal to use when tackling items like fudge, caramel sauce, glazes, or ice cream, where the heavy crystallization that can occur with the monk fruit/erythritol blend can be an issue.

Feel free to use your sweetener of choice if you have a favorite, but pay attention to the notes for best results.

NOTE: Because these sweeteners have no impact on blood sugar, we will not be including the carbohydrates from sugar alcohols or sweeteners in the nutrition facts.

EQUIPMENT

Just as having the right ingredients on hand and ready to go makes keto meals easier to make, having the right equipment in a keto kitchen makes cooking and baking those meals so much easier and more enjoyable. There is nothing fancy here, just a handful of items I can't live without.

- **BLENDER/IMMERSION BLENDER:** I invested in a great quality, high-powered blender more than 10 years ago and it's still going strong. Blenders come in handy for making smoothies, salad dressing, keto coffee, dips, soups, sauces, pancakes, and more! That said, any blender you currently have will work just fine. An immersion blender is also an affordable and useful alternative.

- **CAST-IRON SKILLET:** A good, seasoned, cast-iron skillet is a Southern keto kitchen must-have. From searing steaks and braising chicken and collards to baking cobbler, this versatile skillet can go from stovetop to oven and will literally last a lifetime . . . and then some.

- **STAND MIXER/ELECTRIC HAND MIXER:** Mixers are great for whipping up eggs or whipped cream and a whole mess of keto baked goods. I even use a mixer to shred chicken for chicken salad. A stand mixer is great to have for heavy-duty jobs, but a good electric hand mixer is all you need to create magic in the kitchen.

About the Recipes

I couldn't be more excited to share these Southern keto comfort food recipes and I hope you, your family, and your guests love them as much as my family and friends do! To keep things simple, all the following recipes are labeled for allergens and include macro calculations so you can enjoy all your favorite Southern dishes and stay within your macros. In addition, many recipes have tips for making tasty and simple variations of the recipe to expand your Southern keto recipe repertoire further. These recipes are family-friendly and kid- and Cowboy-approved, and I can promise you even carb lovers will be hollering for seconds!

Some of the happiest times in my life have been spent in kitchens, listening to family tales and absorbing the traditions of my kinfolk. In the following pages you'll find a collection of recipes near and dear to my heart, inspired by the home cooking of some of the strongest, hardworking Texas and Southern women I've had the honor of crossing paths with in this lifetime. Some recipes will be familiar Southern comfort food classics ketofied; some are classic recipes you may recognize with a new twist; and some are brand-new, Southern-inspired keto dishes to keep Southern cuisine and the keto lifestyle fresh, exciting, and delicious.

Wherever you are in your keto journey, I wish you all the best and hope these dishes give you a little taste of that famous Southern hospitality—with a little splash of Texas charm—and inspire you to get in the kitchen, get cooking, and keto on!

Quick and Easy Blueberry Waffles, page 35

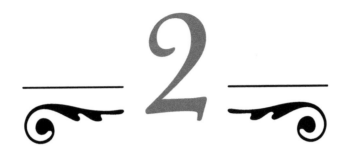

BREAKFAST, BRUNCH, AND BREADS

ORANGE OLIVE OIL POPPY SEED MUFFINS

Dairy-free, Gluten-free, Vegetarian

MAKES 9 MUFFINS / PREP TIME: 15 MINUTES / COOK TIME: 20 MINUTES

Waking up to these orange muffins is a dream come true! The fruity notes of the olive oil lend a sophisticated layer of flavor to this fun breakfast treat.

4 eggs

1 egg yolk

1 cup almond flour

⅓ cup olive oil

6 tablespoons monk fruit/erythritol blend sweetener

¼ cup coconut flour

2 ½ teaspoons baking powder

2 teaspoons grated orange zest

2 teaspoons poppy seeds

¼ teaspoon kosher salt

1 teaspoon vanilla extract

1. Preheat the oven to 350°F. Prepare a standard muffin tin with 9 liners.

2. In the bowl of a stand mixer fitted with the whisk attachment, or in a large bowl and using an electric hand mixer, whip the eggs and egg yolk for about 2 minutes until light and foamy. Add the almond flour, olive oil, sweetener, coconut flour, baking powder, orange zest, poppy seeds, salt, and vanilla. Mix on medium speed until well combined, stopping to scrape down the sides of the bowl at least once.

3. Using a cookie scoop or spoon, evenly divide the batter among the prepared muffin cups.

4. Bake for 15 to 20 minutes, or until golden brown on top.

5. Let the muffins cool in the pan for 10 minutes, then transfer to a wire rack to cool completely. Store the muffins at room temperature in an airtight container for up to 3 days, or freeze for up to 1 month.

Nutrition information per serving: Calories: 170; Total Fat: 14g; Protein: 5g; Total Carbs: 6g; Net Carbs: 2g; Fiber: 4g; Sodium: 98mg; Erythritol Carbs: 8g; Macros: 74% Fat; 12% Protein; 14% Carbs

SOUR CREAM CORN BREAD

Gluten-free, Vegetarian

SERVES 9 / PREP TIME: 10 MINUTES / COOK TIME: 30 MINUTES

Corn bread is a Southern staple and perfect to serve with soups, stews, and chili. This keto version is light, fluffy, and moist with the perfect crumbly texture.

5 tablespoons butter, melted, plus more for preparing the pan

1 cup almond flour

2 ½ tablespoons coconut flour

2 ½ teaspoons baking powder

1 teaspoon monk fruit/erythritol blend sweetener

½ teaspoon sea salt

¼ teaspoon baking soda

5 eggs

2 tablespoons sour cream

1. Preheat the oven to 350°F. Thoroughly coat an 8-by-8-inch pan with butter. Set aside.

2. In a medium bowl, stir together the almond and coconut flours, baking powder, sweetener, salt, and baking soda.

3. Using an electric hand mixer, mix in the eggs and sour cream, beating at medium speed until well combined. Stir in the melted butter.

4. Pour the batter into the prepared pan.

5. Bake for 25 to 30 minutes until golden brown and a toothpick inserted into the center comes out clean. Cut into squares and serve warm.

Variation tip: Try jalapeño Cheddar corn bread: In a small skillet over medium heat, melt 2 teaspoons butter. Add 1 jalapeño pepper, seeded and diced. Sauté for 5 minutes until soft. Set aside to cool. Add ¼ teaspoon granulated garlic and ¼ teaspoon onion powder to the dry ingredients in step 2. Prepare the corn bread batter through step 3. Stir in 1 cup shredded sharp Cheddar cheese, the sautéed jalapeño, and 2 tablespoons sliced scallion. Pour the batter into the prepared pan and bake as directed.

Nutrition information per serving: Calories: 157; Total Fat: 13g; Protein: 5g; Total Carbs: 5g; Net Carbs: 2g; Fiber: 3g; Sodium: 226mg; Erythritol Carbs: 0g; Macros: 76% Fat; 12% Protein; 12% Carbs

NANA'S ZUCCHINI BREAD

Gluten-free, Vegetarian

SERVES 12 / PREP TIME: 20 MINUTES / COOK TIME: 1 HOUR

There's nothing that screams comfort food like a loaf of fresh baked quick bread. I always looked forward to Nana's zucchini bread around the end of summer when we had squash running out of our ears! Super moist with the perfect hint of cinnamon and studded with pecans, this keto version is every bit as delicious as the original. Enjoy a slice warm, slathered in butter with your morning cup of coffee!

Nonstick cooking spray

8 eggs

1 cup almond flour

¾ cup coconut flour

⅔ cup grated zucchini

½ cup monk fruit/erythritol blend sweetener

1½ teaspoons baking powder

1 teaspoon baking soda

1 teaspoon ground cinnamon

1 teaspoon vanilla extract

½ teaspoon kosher salt

5 tablespoons plus 1 teaspoon butter, melted

3 tablespoons sour cream

¼ cup chopped pecans

1. Preheat the oven to 350°F. Coat an 8-inch loaf pan with cooking spray and line it with parchment overhanging two sides. Set aside.

2. In the bowl of a stand mixer fitted with the whisk attachment, or in a large bowl and using an electric hand mixer, whip the eggs for about 2 minutes until light and foamy.

3. Add the almond and coconut flours, zucchini, sweetener, baking powder, baking soda, cinnamon, vanilla, and salt. Mix on medium speed until combined, stopping to scrape down sides at least once. Stir in the melted butter and sour cream until combined.

4. Spoon the batter evenly into the prepared loaf pan and smooth the top. Sprinkle the pecans over the batter.

5. Bake for 45 minutes to 1 hour, or until a toothpick inserted in the center comes out clean. If needed, cover the pan loosely with aluminum foil halfway through the baking time to prevent over-browning.

6. Let cool in the pan for 30 minutes. Using the parchment as an aid, transfer the loaf to a wire rack to cool completely. The cooled loaf can be wrapped and refrigerated for up to 5 days, or frozen whole or in slices for up to 1 month.

Nutrition information per serving: Calories: 186; Total Fat: 14g; Protein: 7g; Total Carbs: 8g; Net Carbs: 4g; Fiber: 4g; Sodium: 283mg; Erythritol Carbs: 8g; Macros: 68% Fat; 15% Protein; 17% Carbs

GREENS AND PARMESAN MUFFINS

Gluten-free

SERVES 8 / PREP TIME: 15 MINUTES / COOK TIME: 20 MINUTES

One bite of these flavorful muffins and I'm in love! Loaded with
Southern goodness, like crispy bacon and cooked collard greens, these savory
muffins make breakfast a Southern treat. Perfect for weekly meal prep,
grab one of these flavor-packed muffins on the way out the door and
you'll be going strong all morning long.

FOR THE COLLARDS

1½ tablespoons butter

1½ cup frozen chopped
    collard greens

1 garlic clove, finely minced

FOR THE MUFFINS

4 eggs

½ cup almond flour

¼ cup coconut flour

¼ teaspoon onion powder

¼ teaspoon garlic powder

⅛ teaspoon cayenne pepper

2½ tablespoons butter, melted

2 tablespoons sour cream

2 tablespoons shredded Parmesan
    cheese, plus more for
    topping (optional)

3 crispy cooked bacon slices,
    finely chopped

TO MAKE THE COLLARDS

In a medium sauté pan or skillet over medium heat, melt the butter. Add the
frozen collards and garlic. Sauté for 7 to 10 minutes until tender. Set aside
to cool.

TO MAKE THE MUFFINS

1. Preheat the oven to 350°F. Prepare a standard muffin tin with eight
    liners. Set aside.

2. In the bowl of a stand mixer fitted with the whisk attachment, or in a
    large bowl and using an electric hand mixer, whip the eggs for about
    2 minutes until light and foamy. Add the almond and coconut flours,

onion powder, garlic powder, cayenne, melted butter, and sour cream. Mix on medium speed until combined, stopping to scrape down the sides at least once.

3. Stir in the Parmesan cheese, bacon, and cooled collard greens.

4. Using a cookie scoop or spoon, evenly divide the batter among the prepared muffin cups. Top the muffins with additional Parmesan, if desired.

5. Bake for 15 to 20 minutes, or until the tops are golden brown.

6. Let the muffins cool in the pan for 10 minutes, then transfer to a wire rack to cool completely. Refrigerate the muffins in an airtight container for up to 4 days.

Time-saving tip: Keeping frozen greens, like collards and kale, on hand for recipes saves a ton of prep time and you can use just the amount you need with no waste.

Nutrition information per serving: Calories: 190; Total Fat: 14g; Protein: 8g; Total Carbs: 8g; Net Carbs: 4g; Fiber: 4g; Sodium: 242mg; Macros: 66% Fat; 17% Protein; 17% Carbs

SOUTHERN DROP BISCUITS AND JALAPEÑO SAUSAGE GRAVY

Gluten-free

MAKES 9 MEDIUM BISCUITS AND ABOUT 1½ CUPS GRAVY /
PREP TIME: 15 MINUTES / COOK TIME: 20 MINUTES

A Southern cookbook would not be complete without biscuits and gravy. These biscuits are light and fluffy on the inside and crisp, buttery, and golden brown on the outside—and topped with this easy Jalapeño Sausage Gravy? Keto perfection!

FOR THE BISCUITS

1½ cups almond flour

2½ tablespoons coconut flour

1 tablespoon baking powder

1½ teaspoons monk fruit/erythritol blend sweetener

½ teaspoon kosher salt

2 eggs, lightly beaten

2 tablespoons sour cream

5 tablespoons butter, melted

FOR THE GRAVY

8 ounces pork sausage

1 or 2 jalapeño peppers, seeded, ribbed, and finely diced (see Preparation tip)

2 tablespoons finely diced onion

2 ounces cream cheese, at room temperature

½ cup unsweetened almond milk

¾ cup heavy (whipping) cream

Kosher salt

Freshly ground black pepper

TO MAKE THE BISCUITS

1. Preheat the oven to 425°F. Line a large sheet pan with parchment paper. Set aside.

2. In a medium bowl, stir together the almond and coconut flours, baking powder, sweetener, and salt. Add the eggs and sour cream and stir well to combine. Pour in the melted butter and stir until fully incorporated.

3. Using a small cookie scoop or a spoon, drop two scoops of dough for each biscuit, placing one scoop of dough on top of the other so you have some height. Flatten the tops of the biscuits slightly, until the dough is between ½ and 1 inch thick. You should get about nine medium biscuits.

4. Bake for about 10 minutes or until the tops are golden brown. Serve warm with the gravy.

TO MAKE THE GRAVY

1. In a large sauté pan or skillet over medium heat, cook the sausage for about 5 minutes until brown. When the sausage is just about cooked through, but still a little pink, add the jalapeño and onion. Continue to cook for 5 minutes more until the sausage begins to caramelize and the vegetables are tender.

2. If there are any brown bits or a brown crust on the bottom of the pan from cooking the sausage, add 3 tablespoons of water to the pan and scrape up the brown bits using a spatula.

3. Add the cream cheese and almond milk. Cook for 2 to 3 minutes, stirring constantly, until the cheese is completely melted.

4. Add the heavy cream and simmer the mixture for about 5 minutes until thickened. Season with salt and pepper.

Allergen tip: For lactose-free biscuits, prepare the dough using ghee instead of butter, omit the sour cream, and use only 2 tablespoons almond milk.

Preparation tip: I like to test the heat level of my jalapeños before I add them to the gravy. Use ½ to 2 jalapeños, depending on their heat level, and how spicy you want your gravy.

Nutrition information per serving: Calories: 352; Total Fat: 32g; Protein: 9g; Total Carbs: 7g; Net Carbs: 4g; Fiber: 3g; Sodium: 395mg; Erythritol Carbs: 0g; Macros: 82% Fat; 10% Protein; 8% Carbs

CINNAMON "APPLE" PECAN COFFEE CAKE

Gluten-free, Vegetarian

SERVES 12 / PREP TIME: 15 MINUTES / COOK TIME: 35 MINUTES

As a child, I remember coffee cakes were always reserved as a treat for mornings when we had guests. To keep this keto friendly, I use chayote squash as a delicious substitute for apples. Sautéed with pecans in butter, sweetener, and warm spices, close your eyes, and you'd think you had a mouthful of juicy apples.

FOR THE "APPLE" TOPPING

3 tablespoons butter

1 chayote squash, peeled and diced

¼ cup allulose blend sweetener

½ teaspoon ground cinnamon

⅛ teaspoon ground cloves

⅛ teaspoon ground nutmeg

⅓ cup chopped pecans

FOR THE COFFEE CAKE

Nonstick cooking spray

1½ cups almond flour

¼ cup plus 2 tablespoons coconut flour

¼ cup monk fruit/erythritol blend sweetener

1 tablespoon baking powder

½ teaspoon ground cinnamon

½ teaspoon kosher salt

3 eggs

½ cup unsweetened almond milk

2 teaspoons vanilla extract

¼ cup sour cream

6 tablespoons butter, melted

TO MAKE THE "APPLE" TOPPING

In a sauté pan or skillet over medium heat, melt the butter. Add the squash and sauté for about 7 minutes, or until the squash is tender. Stir in the sweetener, cinnamon, cloves, nutmeg, and pecans. Cook for 2 to 3 minutes more until the sweetener is dissolved and syrupy. Remove from the heat.

TO MAKE THE COFFEE CAKE

1. Preheat the oven to 350°F. Lightly coat a 9-by-9-inch pan with cooking spray and set aside.

2. In a large bowl and using an electric hand mixer, mix the almond and coconut flours, sweetener, baking powder, cinnamon, and salt until combined.

3. One at a time, add the eggs and mix well after each addition. Add the almond milk and vanilla, and mix until combined. Stir in the sour cream and melted butter to combine. Pour the batter into the prepared pan and spread it evenly.

4. Evenly distribute the squash mixture over the top of the batter and drizzle the syrup from the pan over the top.

5. Bake for 20 to 25 minutes, or until a toothpick inserted into the center comes out clean. Let cool completely before slicing and serving.

Nutrition information per serving: Calories: 210; Total Fat: 18g; Protein: 5g; Total Carbs: 7g; Net Carbs: 4g; Fiber: 3g; Sodium: 196mg; Erythritol Carbs: 8g; Macros: 77% Fat; 10% Protein; 13% Carbs

ONION CHEDDAR BREAD

Gluten-free, Vegetarian

SERVES 12 / PREP TIME: 15 MINUTES / COOK TIME: 42 MINUTES

This savory keto bread pays homage to the South's prized Vidalia onion. Sweet, caramelized onion pairs perfectly with sharp Cheddar in this loaf to make a bread that's perfect for eating alongside—or dipping in—any bowl of soup or stew.

2 tablespoons butter, plus more for preparing the pan

½ cup chopped Vidalia onion

8 eggs

1 cup almond flour

½ cup coconut flour

2 teaspoons baking powder

1 teaspoon baking soda

½ teaspoon kosher salt

¼ teaspoon onion powder

¼ teaspoon garlic powder

¼ teaspoon freshly ground black pepper

⅛ teaspoon cayenne pepper

5 tablespoons butter, melted

2 tablespoons sour cream

1 cup shredded sharp Cheddar cheese

1. Preheat the oven to 350°F. Coat an 8-inch loaf pan with butter and line it with parchment paper overhanging two sides. Set aside.

2. In a small sauté pan or skillet over medium heat, melt the butter. Add the onion and sauté for 7 to 10 minutes until translucent and the onion begins to caramelize.

3. In the bowl of a stand mixer fitted with the whisk attachment, or in a large bowl and using an electric hand mixer, whip the eggs for about 2 minutes until light and foamy. Add the almond and coconut flours, baking powder, baking soda, salt, onion powder, garlic powder, black pepper, and cayenne. Mix on medium speed until combined, stopping to scrape down the sides at least once.

4. Add the melted butter and sour cream and mix well to combine. Stir in the Cheddar cheese and cooked onion.

5. Spoon the batter evenly into the prepared loaf pan and smooth the top.

6. Bake for 45 to 55 minutes, or until a tester inserted into the center comes out clean.

7. Let cool in the pan for 30 minutes. Using the parchment as an aid, transfer the loaf to a wire rack to cool completely.

Variation tip: For onion Cheddar grilled cheese dippers: Preheat a small skillet over medium heat. Take two ½-inch-thick slices of Onion Cheddar Bread and sandwich one slice of Colby cheese between them. Butter both sides of the sandwich and place it in the hot skillet. Cook for 2 to 3 minutes, or until the first side is golden and toasty. Flip and cook the other side for 2 to 3 minutes more. Cut the sandwich into three pieces and serve with a warm bowl of soup.

Nutrition information per serving: Calories: 218; Total Fat: 18g; Protein: 8g; Total Carbs: 6g; Net Carbs: 3g; Fiber: 3g; Sodium: 366mg; Macros: 74% Fat; 15% Protein; 11% Carbs

BANANA BREAD BLENDER PANCAKES

Less than 30 Minutes, Dairy-free, Gluten-free, Vegetarian

SERVES 2 / PREP TIME: 10 MINUTES / COOK TIME: 10 MINUTES

Pancakes are a breakfast favorite around our house, and these blender pancakes are always a hit. We've taken out the carb-y banana and replaced it with banana extract and zucchini . . . don't worry, the kids will never know!

2 eggs

½ cup diced zucchini

¼ cup creamy almond butter, well stirred

1 tablespoon coconut flour

2 teaspoons monk fruit/erythritol blend sweetener

¾ teaspoon ground cinnamon

¾ teaspoon banana extract

½ teaspoon vanilla extract

½ teaspoon baking powder

¼ teaspoon kosher salt

Coconut oil spray, or your favorite nonstick spray

1½ tablespoons finely chopped toasted pecans, divided, plus more for serving

Sugar-free syrup, for serving

1. In a blender, combine the eggs, zucchini, almond butter, coconut flour, sweetener, cinnamon, banana extract, vanilla, baking powder, and salt. Blend until smooth and silky.

2. Coat a griddle pan with coconut spray and preheat it over medium heat.

3. Pour about ¼ cup of batter onto the griddle for each pancake. Turn the heat to medium-low and cook the pancakes slowly for 2 to 3 minutes until bubbles form on the surface and begin to burst around the edges. Sprinkle about 1 teaspoon pecans over each pancake. Using a spatula, carefully flip the pancakes and cook for about 1 minute on the second side. Repeat until all the batter is used. This recipe yields about four pancakes.

4. Serve warm with sugar-free syrup and more chopped pecans. Refrigerate cooked pancakes in an airtight container for up to 4 days.

Nutrition information per serving: Calories: 350; Total Fat: 26g; Protein: 15g; Total Carbs: 14g; Net Carbs: 6g; Fiber: 8g; Sodium: 466mg; Erythritol Carbs: 4g; Macros: 67% Fat; 17% Protein; 16% Carbs

COUNTRY GARDEN SCRAMBLE

30 Minutes, Gluten-free, Nut-free, Vegetarian

SERVES 4 / PREP TIME: 20 MINUTES / COOK TIME: 10 MINUTES

Scrambles are my go-to for a quick breakfast on a busy morning. Loaded with a mess of vegetables and topped with melty Fontina, this scramble is a family favorite. Feel free to use whatever veggies you have on hand.

8 eggs

¼ cup sour cream

1 tablespoon chopped fresh parsley

½ teaspoon kosher salt, divided

¼ teaspoon freshly ground
   black pepper

4 tablespoons butter, divided

1 cup diced zucchini

½ cup chopped asparagus

¼ cup diced red bell pepper

2 tablespoons sliced scallion

1 cup fresh baby spinach

½ cup shredded Fontina cheese

1. In a large bowl, whisk together the eggs, sour cream, parsley, ¼ teaspoon of salt, and pepper. Set aside.

2. In a large sauté pan or skillet over medium heat, melt 2 tablespoons of butter. Add the zucchini, asparagus, red bell pepper, and remaining ¼ teaspoon of salt. Sauté for about 5 minutes until tender. Add the spinach and scallion. Cook for 1 minute just until the spinach wilts.

3. Turn the heat to medium-low and add the remaining 2 tablespoons of butter to the pan to melt.

4. Pour the egg mixture into the pan. Cook the eggs, without stirring, for about 2 minutes until they start to set on the bottom of the skillet. Using a rubber spatula, scrape the cooked eggs from the bottom of the pan forming curds while mixing the veggies into the eggs. Cook for about 2 minutes more until the eggs are cooked and firm, but still glossy and moist. Remove from the heat and sprinkle the Fontina cheese over the top. Serve immediately.

Nutrition information per serving: Calories: 332; Total Fat: 28g; Protein: 16g; Total Carbs: 4g; Net Carbs: 3g; Fiber: 1g; Sodium: 522mg; Macros: 76% Fat; 19% Protein; 5% Carbs

CHICKEN BRUNCH PIE
WITH CHEDDAR PECAN CRUST

....

Gluten-free

SERVES 8 / PREP TIME: 20 MINUTES / COOK TIME: 1 HOUR

Creamy, dreamy chicken filling paired with a savory crust studded with pecans and Cheddar. This dish is insanely delish and perfect for any meal. Chicken Brunch Pie is soul satisfying and, paired with a simple salad, a definite crowd-pleaser. And don't say I didn't warn you: If you're looking forward to leftovers, you better make extra!

....

FOR THE CRUST

1½ cups almond flour

¼ cup pecans, finely chopped

⅓ cup shredded sharp
    Cheddar cheese

¼ teaspoon freshly ground
    black pepper

Pinch kosher salt

3 tablespoons butter, melted

FOR THE FILLING

1 cup sour cream

¼ cup mayonnaise

4 eggs

¾ teaspoon kosher salt

¼ teaspoon freshly ground
    black pepper

¼ teaspoon paprika

2 cups chopped cooked chicken

½ cup shredded sharp
    Cheddar cheese

3 scallions, sliced

TO MAKE THE CRUST

1. Preheat the oven to 350°F.

2. In a small bowl, stir together the almond flour, pecans, Cheddar cheese, pepper, and salt. Pour in the melted butter and stir until thoroughly incorporated. The mixture will be crumbly. Firmly press the crust mixture evenly into the bottom and up the sides of a 9-inch pie plate.

3. Bake for 12 to 15 minutes, or until the edges are golden brown. Leave the oven on.

TO MAKE THE FILLING

1. In a medium bowl, whisk the sour cream, mayonnaise, eggs, salt, pepper, and paprika until blended. Stir in the chicken, Cheddar cheese, and scallions, stirring until thoroughly combined. Pour the mixture into the baked piecrust.

2. Bake for 40 to 45 minutes, or until set. If needed, cover lightly with aluminum foil to prevent over-browning.

3. Let cool for at least 20 minutes before slicing. This savory pie is best served warm or at room temperature.

Time-saving tip: Use leftover cooked chicken, or even a rotisserie chicken, for super-quick meal prep.

Nutrition information per serving: Calories: 369; Total Fat: 29g; Protein: 20g; Total Carbs: 7g; Net Carbs: 5g; Fiber: 2g; Sodium: 461mg; Macros: 71% Fat; 22% Protein; 7% Carbs

CRUSTLESS SAUSAGE AND GREEN CHILE QUICHE

Gluten-free, Nut-free

SERVES 8 / PREP TIME: 15 MINUTES / COOK TIME: 35 MINUTES

Even as a child I was a huge fan of quiche. For me, it was all about the velvety, creamy texture of the eggs. The simple combination of green chilies and sausage gives this quiche amazing flavor with only a few ingredients, which means preparation could not be easier. And, it's so good, you'll never miss the crust.

Nonstick cooking spray

1 pound cooked pork
    breakfast sausage

1 (7-ounce) can mild chopped
    green chilies

1 cup shredded Monterey Jack
    cheese, divided

6 eggs

3 ounces cream cheese,
    at room temperature

½ cup sour cream

¼ cup heavy (whipping) cream

½ teaspoon kosher salt

¼ teaspoon freshly ground
    black pepper

1. Preheat the oven to 350°F. Lightly coat a 9-inch pie plate with cooking spray. Set aside.

2. In a medium bowl, stir together the cooked sausage, green chilies, and ½ cup Monterey Jack cheese. Evenly spread the sausage mixture into the bottom of the prepared pie plate.

3. In a blender, combine the eggs, cream cheese, sour cream, heavy cream, salt, and pepper. Blend on low speed until well combined. Alternatively, this can be done in a bowl with a whisk; make sure your ingredients are at room temperature. Pour the egg mixture over the sausage and sprinkle the remaining Monterey Jack cheese evenly over the top.

4. Bake for 35 to 45 minutes, or until set. Cover lightly with foil to prevent over-browning.

5. Let cool for at least 20 minutes before serving.

Variation tip: If you like your breakfast with a kick, substitute pepper Jack cheese for the Monterey Jack to amp up the spice factor.

Nutrition information per serving: Calories: 417; Total Fat: 37g; Protein: 17g; Total Carbs: 4g; Net Carbs: 3g; Fiber: 1g; Sodium: 657mg; Macros: 80% Fat; 16% Protein; 4% Carbs

CHORIZO EGG MUFFINS

Gluten-free, Nut-free

MAKES 12 MUFFINS / PREP TIME: 10 MINUTES / COOK TIME: 32 MINUTES

Chorizo and egg breakfast tacos are a staple in south Texas and one of my favorite breakfast flavor combos. Mexican chorizo is a heavily spiced, fresh sausage found in the grocery store's refrigerated section. It's most often found in a plastic casing that must be removed before cooking. It can then be broken up and cooked like traditional pork sausage.

Nonstick cooking spray

12 ounces Mexican chorizo, casing removed

1½ cups shredded Monterey Jack cheese, divided

6 eggs

2 ounces cream cheese, at room temperature

2 tablespoons sour cream

1½ tablespoons salsa

½ teaspoon kosher salt

¼ teaspoon freshly ground black pepper

1. Preheat the oven to 325°F. Liberally coat a standard muffin tin with cooking spray. Set aside.

2. In a large sauté pan or skillet over medium-high heat, cook the chorizo for 7 to 10 minutes, breaking it up into crumbles with a spoon or spatula, until thoroughly cooked. Using a spoon, evenly divide the cooked chorizo among the prepared muffin cups.

3. Evenly divide the Monterey Jack cheese among the cups, about 2 tablespoons in each.

4. In a blender, combine the eggs, cream cheese, sour cream, salsa, salt, and pepper. Blend until combined. Evenly divide the egg mixture among the muffin cups, pouring it over the cheese and chorizo.

5. Bake for 20 to 25 minutes, or until set.

6. Let the muffins cool in the pan for at least 20 minutes before removing them. Run a butter knife around each muffin to loosen it from the pan. Serve warm or at room temperature. Refrigerate in an airtight container for up to 4 days.

Troubleshooting tip: Eggs are notorious for sticking when baked, so I like to use a lightly sprayed silicone muffin pan to bake these egg muffins in. When I do, I have no problems removing them. Parchment muffin pan liners also work great in a pinch.

Nutrition information per serving: Calories: 240; Total Fat: 20g; Protein: 14g; Total Carbs: 1g; Net Carbs: 1g; Fiber: 0g; Sodium: 592mg; Macros: 75% Fat; 23% Protein; 2% Carbs

CINNAMON ROLL "NOATMEAL"

Less than 30 Minutes, Gluten-free, Vegetarian

SERVES 2 / PREP TIME: 15 MINUTES / COOK TIME: 10 MINUTES

When the sweltering Southern summers come to an end and the first cold front hits, I crave a warm, comforting breakfast. This "noatmeal" is the perfect keto-friendly substitute for traditional oatmeal, with coconut flakes and toasted pecans providing great texture and crunch.

2 tablespoons butter

2 tablespoons chopped pecans

¼ cup almond flour

1½ teaspoons coconut flour

¼ cup unsweetened almond milk, plus more as needed

Pinch kosher salt

2 tablespoons hemp seeds

1 tablespoon desiccated unsweetened coconut

1 tablespoon monk fruit/erythritol blend sweetener

1½ teaspoons golden flax meal

¼ teaspoon ground cinnamon

1 tablespoon heavy (whipping) cream (optional)

1. In a small saucepan over medium-low heat, combine the butter and pecans. Cook for 3 to 4 minutes until the butter is golden brown and the pecans are toasted.

2. Stir in the almond and coconut flours, almond milk, and salt. Cook for 3 to 4 minutes until thickened.

3. Stir in the hemp seeds, coconut, sweetener, flax meal, and cinnamon. Cook for 1 to 2 minutes more. Remove from the heat and stir in the heavy cream (if using). Add additional almond milk, as needed, to reach your desired consistency. Serve immediately.

Allergy tip: To make this hearty breakfast lactose-free, use ghee in place of the butter. Note that ghee will not brown quite like butter but will help toast the pecans.

Nutrition information per serving: Calories: 334; Total Fat: 29g; Protein: 10g; Total Carbs: 8g; Net Carbs: 3g; Fiber: 5g; Sodium: 185mg; Erythritol Carbs: 6g; Macros: 78% Fat; 12% Protein; 10% Carbs

QUICK AND EASY BLUEBERRY WAFFLES

Gluten-free, Vegetarian

SERVES 6 / PREP TIME: 5 MINUTES / COOK TIME: 5 MINUTES PER WAFFLE

Waffles are one of Maddie's favorite breakfast treats, and these blueberry-studded waffles are the bee's knees! The batter comes together in minutes, which means breakfast can be on the table in no time flat.

1 cup almond flour

¼ cup coconut flour

¼ cup monk fruit/erythritol blend sweetener

2½ teaspoons baking powder

¼ teaspoon kosher salt

4 eggs, slightly beaten

5 tablespoons plus 1 teaspoon butter, melted

2 tablespoons sour cream

1 teaspoon vanilla extract

½ cup frozen blueberries, thawed

1. Preheat a traditional waffle iron to high heat and prepare it according to the manufacturer's instructions.

2. In a medium bowl, stir together the almond and coconut flours, sweetener, baking powder, and salt.

3. In a small bowl, whisk the eggs, melted butter, sour cream, and vanilla until combined. Add these wet ingredients to the dry ingredients and whisk until thoroughly combined.

4. Gently stir in the blueberries, breaking them up into the batter.

5. To the preheated waffle iron, add about ½ cup of batter and close the iron. Cook for 3 to 5 minutes, or until golden brown. Remove. Repeat with the remaining batter.

Variation tip: Preheat the oven to 350°F. Make batter as directed and stir in ½ teaspoon grated lemon zest with the sour cream. Evenly divide the batter among 12 standard lined muffin cups. Bake for 18 to 20 minutes, or until golden.

Nutrition information per serving: Calories: 240; Total Fat: 20g; Protein: 7g; Total Carbs: 8g; Net Carbs: 4g; Fiber: 4g; Sodium: 219mg; Erythritol Carbs: 8g; Macros: 75% Fat; 12% Protein; 13% Carbs

Green Chile Deviled Eggs, page 41

3

APPETIZERS AND SNACKS

JALAPEÑO MEXICAN FUDGE

Gluten-free, Vegetarian

SERVES 16 / PREP TIME: 15 MINUTES / COOK TIME: 35 MINUTES

**I like to describe this treat as a savory nacho cheese fat bomb with
a crusty caramelized top, soft cheesy insides, and a spicy jalapeño kick.
Does it get any better?**

Nonstick cooking spray

6 ounces pickled, sliced jalapeño
  peppers, drained and
  roughly chopped

1 pound Cheddar cheese
  (mild or medium), grated

1 pound Monterey Jack
  cheese, grated

3 extra-large eggs, beaten

¼ cup heavy (whipping) cream

2 tablespoons unsweetened
  almond milk

¼ teaspoon garlic powder

⅛ teaspoon onion powder

1. Preheat the oven to 350°F. Lightly coat a 9-by-9-inch baking dish with
   cooking spray. Set aside.

2. Spread the jalapeños across the bottom of the prepared baking dish in a
   single layer. Taste your jalapeños and use less, as desired.

3. In a large bowl, mix the Cheddar and Monterey Jack cheeses, eggs, heavy
   cream, almond milk, garlic powder, and onion powder to combine. I find
   it easiest to use my hands. Pour the cheese mixture over the jalapeños
   and spread it evenly.

4. Bake for 30 to 35 minutes, or until golden brown and bubbly. Cool
   completely in the pan before cutting. Best served slightly warm or at
   room temperature.

Variation tip: If you're not a fan of hot and spicy foods, substitute chopped mild
green chiles for the jalapeños in this cheesy appetizer recipe.

Nutrition information per serving: Calories: 249; Total Fat: 21g; Protein: 14g; Total Carbs: 1g; Net
Carbs: 1g; Fiber: 0g; Sodium: 539mg; Macros: 76% Fat; 22% Protein; 2% Carbs

CLASSIC SOUTHERN PIMIENTO CHEESE

Less than 30 Minutes, Gluten-free, Nut-free, Vegetarian

MAKES 4 CUPS / PREP TIME: 10 MINUTES / COOK TIME: 10 MINUTES

My preferred way to enjoy this cheesy spread is on cool cucumber slices or celery sticks but for a real treat, place a dollop on a grilled burger patty.

2 cups finely shredded mild Cheddar cheese

2 cups finely shredded Monterey Jack cheese

1 cup finely shredded sharp Cheddar cheese

1 teaspoon freshly ground black pepper

1 teaspoon grated onion

½ teaspoon granulated garlic

1 (4-ounce) jar diced pimientos

¾ to 1 cup mayonnaise

2 to 4 dashes hot sauce

1. In a large bowl, toss together the mild Cheddar, Monterey Jack, and sharp Cheddar cheeses, pepper, onion, and garlic, distributing the seasonings.

2. Stir in the pimientos, mayonnaise, and hot sauce, mixing thoroughly. I like to mix this with my hands, using gloves, so I can get all the ingredients combined well. Refrigerate for a few hours, or overnight, for the best flavor. The pimiento cheese will tighten up as it sits and you may have to stir in a tablespoon of mayo to get it to the consistency you like. Refrigerate in an airtight container for up to 4 days.

Variation tip: For jalapeño pimiento cheese, preheat the oven to 450°F. Place 2 or 3 whole jalapeño peppers on a parchment paper–lined baking sheet. Roast for 10 to 15 minutes, turning once. The peppers are done when blistered and charred and the skins start to split. Place the peppers in a bowl and cover with plastic wrap to cool. When cool, wearing gloves, stem the peppers and split lengthwise to remove the seeds. Finely chop the roasted jalapeños and add them a tablespoon at a time to the cheese mixture with the pimientos until you reach your desired heat level.

Nutrition information per serving (¼ cup): Calories: 246; Total Fat: 22g; Protein: 9g; Total Carbs: 3g; Net Carbs: 3g; Fiber: 0g; Sodium: 310mg; Macros: 80% Fat; 15% Protein; 5% Carbs

PECAN CHICKEN SALAD

Dairy-free, Gluten-free

SERVES 12 / PREP TIME: 15 MINUTES / CHILL TIME: 2 HOURS

During the hot summer months, you can bet there is always a batch of this chicken salad in my refrigerator. In my restaurant days it was a best seller and a most-requested recipe. Perfect for wrapping in lettuce or served in a tomato or avocado cup, this quick and easy salad is great to pack for lunch or have on hand for an effortless dinner.

4 cups shredded cooked chicken

1 cup finely diced celery

¾ cup chopped pecans, lightly toasted

¼ cup sliced scallion

1 to 1½ cups mayonnaise

1 tablespoon freshly squeezed lemon juice

2 teaspoons celery salt

1 teaspoon freshly ground black pepper

1. In a large bowl, toss together the chicken, celery, pecans, and scallion.

2. In a small bowl, stir together the mayonnaise, lemon juice, celery salt, and pepper until thoroughly combined. Pour the mayonnaise mixture over the chicken and toss to combine. Cover and chill for at least 1 to 2 hours before serving. The chicken salad will firm up in the refrigerator as everything absorbs. You may have to add more mayo, as needed, to reach your desired consistency.

How-to tip: To toast pecans, place the pecan pieces in a heavy-bottomed skillet over medium-low heat. Cook, stirring frequently, until the nuts are fragrant and toasted. Transfer the nuts to a bowl to cool. Don't walk away from nuts on the stove! They can burn quickly.

Nutrition information per serving (½ cup): Calories: 248; Total Fat: 20g; Protein: 15g; Total Carbs: 2g; Net Carbs: 1g; Fiber: 1g; Sodium: 158mg; Macros: 73% Fat; 24% Protein; 3% Carbs

GREEN CHILE DEVILED EGGS

Less than 30 Minutes, Gluten-free, Nut-free

SERVES 12 / PREP TIME: 10 MINUTES / COOK TIME: 10 MINUTES

Deviled eggs are a popular snack or appetizer at any Southern gathering, but these are not your grandma's stuffed eggs! This version uses some green chilies, a little cream cheese, and a dash of hot sauce to add an unexpected twist to this classic dish.

6 hard-boiled eggs, peeled and halved lengthwise

3 ounces cream cheese, at room temperature

2½ tablespoons mayonnaise

2½ tablespoons canned mild green chilies

¼ teaspoon kosher salt

½ teaspoon Worcestershire sauce

⅛ teaspoon garlic powder

3 or 4 drops hot sauce

2 crispy cooked bacon slices, chopped

1. Using a small spoon, scoop the egg yolks into a small bowl. Using a fork, break up the yolks, mashing them. Add the cream cheese and mayonnaise and continue to mash until smooth. Stir in the green chilies, salt, Worcestershire sauce, garlic powder, and hot sauce. Spoon or pipe the egg yolk mixture into the egg whites.

2. Top each with crispy bacon. Refrigerate until serving.

Nutrition information per serving (2 halves): Calories: 172; Total Fat: 16g; Protein: 6g; Total Carbs: 1g; Net Carbs: 1g; Fiber: 0g; Sodium: 427mg; Macros: 84% Fat; 14% Protein; 2% Carbs

SPICY CHEDDAR WAFERS

Egg-free, Gluten-free, Vegetarian

MAKES 30 WAFERS / PREP TIME: 10 MINUTES / CHILL TIME: 2 HOURS /
COOK TIME: 25 MINUTES

Sometimes, nothing but a cracker will do and these Cheddar wafers are a tasty keto cracker alternative. The dough is like slice-and-bake cookies and can be kept in the freezer or refrigerator until needed. When I make a batch of these, I can't keep up with the hands snagging them off the baking sheets as they cool!

1 cup almond flour

2 tablespoons coconut flour

¼ teaspoon kosher salt

¼ teaspoon cayenne pepper

¼ teaspoon garlic powder

¼ teaspoon onion powder

5 tablespoons butter,
at room temperature

1 ounce cream cheese,
at room temperature

4 ounces sharp Cheddar
cheese, shredded

¼ cup finely chopped pecans

1. In a small bowl, stir together the almond and coconut flours, salt, cayenne, garlic powder, and onion powder. Set aside.

2. In a large bowl and using an electric hand mixer, cream together the butter and cream cheese. Add the Cheddar cheese, and mix until well combined. Add the almond flour mixture and mix to combine. Stir in the chopped pecans. Place the dough on plastic wrap or parchment paper and form it into a roll about 2½ inches thick. Wrap the dough tightly and refrigerate until firm, at least 2 hours.

3. Preheat the oven to 300°F. Line a baking sheet with parchment paper.

4. Slice the chilled dough into ¼-inch-thick slices and place them on the prepared baking sheet.

5. Bake for 20 to 25 minutes, or until lightly golden brown. Cool the crackers completely on the pan before removing.

Variation tip: For a new flavor combination, try nutty Gruyère cheese in place of the Cheddar and chopped walnuts instead of pecans.

Nutrition information per serving (3 wafers): Calories: 184; Total Fat: 16g; Protein: 6g; Total Carbs: 4g; Net Carbs: 2g; Fiber: 2g; Sodium: 180mg; Macros: 78% Fat; 13% Protein; 9% Carbs

TEXAS TRASH

Egg-free, Gluten-free

SERVES 10 TO 12 / PREP TIME: 15 MINUTES / COOK TIME: 1 HOUR, 15 MINUTES

This snack mix is usually made with carb-y ingredients like pretzels and cereal, and is traditionally a must-have around the holidays, at least in our house. My mom always made giant batches of this fun mix and kept a big jar on the counter for visitors and always sent a goodie bag home with guests. Well, this keto version hits all the notes—savory, salty, spicy—and can be enjoyed all year long.

1½ (5-ounce) bags pork rinds, broken into bite-size pieces

½ cup raw almonds

½ cup raw pecans

½ cup raw Brazil nuts

6 tablespoons melted butter

2 tablespoons Worcestershire sauce

2 teaspoons hot sauce or sriracha

½ teaspoon onion powder

½ teaspoon garlic powder

½ teaspoon paprika

½ teaspoon kosher salt

¼ teaspoon celery salt

1½ cups Cheddar cheese crisps, purchased or homemade

1. Preheat the oven to 250°F. Line a large sheet pan with parchment paper. Set aside.

2. In a large bowl, mix the pork rinds, almonds, pecans, and Brazil nuts.

3. In a small bowl, whisk the melted butter, Worcestershire sauce, hot sauce, onion powder, garlic powder, paprika, salt, and celery salt to combine. Pour the butter mixture over the pork rinds and nuts, and toss to coat. Pour everything onto the prepared sheet pan and spread it evenly.

4. Bake for 1 hour to 1 hour and 15 minutes, stirring every 15 minutes. The pork rinds should be crispy, not soggy.

5. Remove from the oven, add the cheese crisps, and gently toss to incorporate them into the warm mixture. Transfer the Texas Trash onto paper towels to cool. Pack into an airtight container and store at room temperature.

Allergen tip: For a lactose-free Texas Trash, substitute ghee for the melted butter and omit the cheese crisps.

How-to tip: To make your own cheese crisps: Preheat the oven to 400°F. Line a sheet pan with parchment paper. Divide 4 ounces of shredded sharp Cheddar into small mounds on your prepared sheet pan about 2 inches apart. Depending on the size of your pan, you may need to bake them in two batches. Bake for 6 to 8 minutes, or until golden around the edges. Cool completely on the pan before transferring to a paper towel to drain.

Nutrition information per serving (⅓ cup): Calories: 388; Total Fat: 32g; Protein: 21g; Total Carbs: 4g; Net Carbs: 2g; Fiber: 2g; Sodium: 512mg; Macros: 74% Fat; 22% Protein; 4% Carbs

COWBOY CHILI CHEESE DIP

Egg-free, Gluten-free, Nut-free

MAKES ABOUT 3 CUPS / PREP TIME: 15 MINUTES / COOK TIME: 20 MINUTES

If our favorite queso and Texas chili had an amazing flavor bomb of a baby, it would be this Chili Cheese Dip. Warm, rich, and full of Texas flair, this quick and easy dip will be a hit at your next party or game day. We love using pork rinds as a dipper for this delicious treat.

1 pound ground beef

⅓ cup diced onion

3 garlic cloves, finely minced

1½ teaspoons kosher salt, divided

2 tablespoons ancho chile powder

½ teaspoon ground cumin

1½ cups water

2 tablespoons tomato paste

2 ounces cream cheese, at room temperature

1¾ cups shredded medium Cheddar cheese, divided

Sour cream, for garnish

Diced avocado, for garnish

Chopped tomato, for garnish

Black olives, for garnish

Chopped fresh cilantro or parsley, for garnish

1. In a large sauté pan or skillet over medium heat, combine the ground beef, onion, garlic, and ½ teaspoon of salt. Cook for 5 to 7 minutes, or until the meat is no longer pink and begins to caramelize and the onion is tender.

2. Add the chile powder and cumin. Cook for 1 minute more.

3. Stir in the water, tomato paste, and remaining 1 teaspoon of salt. Simmer for 2 to 3 minutes, or until the mixture thickens some. Taste the chili and add more salt, as needed.

4. Stir in the cream cheese until melted. Remove the skillet from the heat and add 1½ cups of Cheddar cheese. Stir until fully incorporated. Pour the chili mixture into a small casserole dish and cover until ready to serve.

5. When ready to serve, preheat the oven to 400°F.

6. Top the chili mixture with the remaining ¼ cup of Cheddar cheese and bake for 7 to 10 minutes, or until bubbly.

7. Garnish as desired for serving.

....

Variation tip: Transform this delicious dip into a kicked-up Mexican baked spaghetti meal. Mix this cheesy, spiced dip with 4 cups cooked spaghetti squash. Place it in a greased casserole dish and top with ½ cup shredded Cheddar cheese. Bake at 400°F for 15 minutes, or until bubbly and the cheese is melted. Top with sliced scallion.

Nutrition information per serving (¼ cup): Calories: 168; Total Fat: 12g; Protein: 13g; Total Carbs: 3g; Net Carbs: 2g; Fiber: 1g; Sodium: 456mg; Macros: 65% Fat; 31% Protein; 4% Carbs

SPICY BARBECUE PECANS

Egg-free, Gluten-free

SERVES 8 / PREP TIME: 15 MINUTES / COOK TIME: 20 MINUTES

These roasted and spiced pecans are easy to make and great to have on hand when only a salty, crunchy snack will do. Pack them in individual-serving bags for a quick grab-and-go snack or pack in lunches for easy macro tracking.

2 ½ tablespoons butter, melted

1 tablespoon gluten-free
   Worcestershire Sauce

1 tablespoon tamari, or gluten-free
   soy sauce

1 teaspoon kosher salt

½ teaspoon chili powder

½ teaspoon garlic powder

¼ teaspoon cayenne pepper

¼ teaspoon dry mustard

2 cups pecan halves

1. Preheat the oven to 325°F. Line a sheet pan with parchment paper. Set aside.

2. In a medium bowl, stir together the melted butter, Worcestershire sauce, tamari, salt, chili powder, garlic powder, cayenne, and mustard.

3. Add the pecans and toss to coat well. Pour the coated pecans on the prepared sheet pan and spread into a single layer.

4. Bake for 18 to 20 minutes, stirring once halfway through the cooking time. Keep a close eye on them to ensure they don't burn.

5. Spread the pecan halves on paper towels to cool completely before packing in an airtight container for storage.

Nutrition information per serving (¼ cup): Calories: 270; Total Fat: 26g; Protein: 4g; Total Carbs: 5g; Net Carbs: 1g; Fiber: 4g; Sodium: 479mg; Macros: 87% Fat; 6% Protein; 7% Carbs

SCALLION SHRIMP DIP

Less than 30 Minutes, Egg-free, Gluten-free, Nut-free

SERVES 12 / PREP TIME: 10 MINUTES / COOK TIME: 10 MINUTES

This is my husband, the Cowboy's, favorite dip of all time. My mom started making this delicious dip years ago and it was a hit with everyone who tasted it. Now when we're invited for dinner or a family party, the first thing the Cowboy asks is, "Is she making shrimp dip?" Well, over the years, I learned her secret and created a keto version that is just as amazing. Served with cucumber slices, keto crackers, or even pork rinds, this dip is a crowd-pleaser.

8 ounces cream cheese, at room temperature

1 tablespoon chopped fresh parsley, or ½ teaspoon dried parsley

½ teaspoon gluten-free Worcestershire sauce

½ teaspoon garlic powder

½ teaspoon onion powder

½ teaspoon kosher salt, plus more for garnish

¼ teaspoon freshly ground black pepper, plus more for garnish

¾ cup sour cream

12 ounces small frozen salad shrimp, thawed, dried, and roughly chopped

¼ cup sliced scallion, plus more for garnish

1. In a large bowl and using an electric hand mixer, beat together the cream cheese, parsley, Worcestershire sauce, garlic powder, onion powder, salt, and pepper.

2. Stir in the sour cream.

3. Gently stir in the shrimp and scallion. Spoon into a serving bowl and refrigerate.

4. Garnish with additional scallion, pepper, and a sprinkle of salt for serving.

Nutrition information per serving: Calories: 130; Total Fat: 10g; Protein: 8g; Total Carbs: 2g; Net Carbs: 2g; Fiber: 0g; Sodium: 232mg; Macros: 69% Fat; 25% Protein; 6% Carbs

SAUSAGE AND SPINACH-STUFFED MUSHROOMS

Egg-free, Gluten-free, Nut-free

SERVES 15 / PREP TIME: 15 MINUTES / COOK TIME: 35 MINUTES

When there's a family gathering, I guarantee there are stuffed mushrooms being served, especially if my grandpa will be there. The version he loves is stuffed with only sausage and Parmesan, but I love the addition of spinach and Fontina for some texture and gooeyness. These stuffed mushrooms are simply stunning served on a platter on a buffet, or make a batch in advance to pair with a salad for a light dinner.

15 whole button mushrooms, or cremini mushrooms, cleaned and stemmed (reserve the stems)

3 tablespoons butter

2 tablespoons finely chopped onion

2 garlic cloves, minced

¼ teaspoon kosher salt

1 cup fresh spinach, chopped

8 ounces spicy pork sausage

1 tablespoon gluten-free Worcestershire sauce

1 tablespoon chopped fresh parsley

⅓ cup shredded Parmesan cheese, plus more for garnish

½ cup shredded Fontina cheese

1. Preheat the oven to 400°F. Line a sheet pan with parchment. Set aside.

2. Finely chop the reserved mushroom stems and set aside.

3. In a sauté pan or skillet over medium to medium-high heat, melt the butter. Add the onion, garlic, mushroom stems, and salt. Cook for 7 to 10 minutes, or until the onion is translucent and soft, and the liquid from the mushroom stems is almost gone.

4. Stir in the spinach and cook for about 2 minutes, just until the spinach wilts. Remove from the heat to cool.

5. In a medium bowl, stir together the sausage, Worcestershire sauce, parsley, and cooled spinach mixture. Add the Parmesan and Fontina cheeses and mix until thoroughly combined.

6. Stuff each mushroom cap with about 1 tablespoon of filling, depending on their size. The filling should be heaping. Arrange the stuffed mushrooms on the prepared sheet pan. Sprinkle with a little Parmesan cheese.

7. Bake for 20 to 25 minutes, or until cooked through and browned. Serve warm or at room temperature.

Nutrition information per serving: Calories: 100; Total Fat: 8g; Protein: 5g; Total Carbs: 2g; Net Carbs: 2g; Fiber: 0g; Sodium: 219mg; Macros: 72% Fat; 20% Protein; 8% Carbs

CHEESY ZUCCHINI BITES

Gluten-free, Vegetarian

MAKES 28 BITES / PREP TIME: 15 MINUTES / COOK TIME: 27 MINUTES

Cheesy Zucchini Bites are a cross between a mini muffin and a quiche, and remind me of a squash casserole my mom used to make when I was a child that I just couldn't get enough of. I love foods that evoke some kind of food memory 'cause that's what comfort food is all about.

1 tablespoon butter, plus more for preparing the muffin pan

1½ cups shredded zucchini

¼ cup diced onion

2 garlic cloves, finely minced

1 teaspoon kosher salt, divided

1 cup almond flour

3 tablespoons coconut flour

2½ teaspoons baking powder

½ teaspoon freshly ground black pepper

½ teaspoon monk fruit/erythritol blend sweetener

¼ teaspoon Italian seasoning

1½ tablespoons finely chopped scallion

3 eggs

4 tablespoons butter, melted

2 tablespoons sour cream

½ cup shredded sharp Cheddar cheese

¼ cup shredded Parmesan cheese

1. Preheat the oven to 350°F. Coat a mini muffin tin with butter, or line it with liners. Set aside. If using a silicone mini muffin pan, coat it well with nonstick cooking spray and set aside.

2. In a sauté pan or skillet over medium heat, melt the butter. Add the zucchini, onion, garlic, and ½ teaspoon of salt. Sauté the vegetables for 5 to 7 minutes, or until the onion is translucent. There should be no liquid left in the pan. Set aside the zucchini mixture to cool.

3. In a large bowl, stir together the almond and coconut flours, the remaining ½ teaspoon of salt, the baking powder, pepper, sweetener, Italian seasoning, and scallion.

4. One at a time, stir in the eggs.

5. Stir in the melted butter, sour cream, and the cooled zucchini mixture, and mix well. Stir in the Cheddar and Parmesan cheeses.

6. Using a cookie scoop or spoon, fill the prepared mini muffin pan using about 1 tablespoon for each zucchini bite.

7. Bake for 20 minutes, or until the tops are just golden brown. Cool in the pan for 5 minutes, then remove from pan and cool completely on a wire rack. These bites can be served warm or at room temperature.

Variation tip: Feeling fancy or serving these mini appetizers for a dinner party? Dress them up by subbing Gruyère cheese for the Cheddar.

Nutrition information per serving (3 bites): Calories: 191; Total Fat: 15g; Protein: 7g; Total Carbs: 7g; Net Carbs: 4g; Fiber: 3g; Sodium: 401mg; Erythritol Carbs: 0g; Macros: 71% Fat; 15% Protein; 14% Carbs

OVEN-FRIED GREEN TOMATOES WITH AVOCADO RANCH

Gluten-free, Vegetarian

SERVES 6; MAKES ABOUT 1⅓ CUPS AVOCADO RANCH / PREP TIME: 15 MINUTES / CHILL TIME: 1 HOUR / COOK TIME: 10 MINUTES

Fried green tomatoes are one of the first things that come to mind when I think about Southern cuisine. These green tomatoes are oven-fried to make cooking and cleanup a breeze. A blend of almond flour and Parmesan is used for the breading, creating a crust that browns nicely in the oven and complements the tasty green tomatoes perfectly. Serve warm for dipping in the avocado ranch—it's a match made in keto heaven!

FOR THE AVOCADO RANCH

½ cup mayonnaise

½ cup unsweetened almond milk

⅓ cup avocado

1 garlic clove, peeled

2 teaspoons gluten-free Worcestershire sauce

1 teaspoon Creole mustard

½ teaspoon kosher salt

¼ teaspoon onion powder

1½ teaspoons dried parsley

½ teaspoon Italian seasoning

FOR THE FRIED GREEN TOMATOES

½ cup grated Parmesan cheese

¼ cup almond flour

¼ teaspoon freshly ground black pepper

¼ teaspoon garlic powder

¼ teaspoon paprika

¼ teaspoon kosher salt

⅛ teaspoon cayenne pepper

1 tablespoon unsweetened almond milk

1 large egg, lightly beaten

3 green tomatoes, sliced

TO MAKE THE AVOCADO RANCH

1. In a blender, combine the mayo, almond milk, avocado, garlic, Worcestershire sauce, mustard, salt, and onion powder. Blend on high speed until smooth.

2. Add the dried parsley and Italian seasoning, and stir to combine, or blend on low speed until just mixed. Refrigerate for at least 1 hour before serving. Store in an airtight container or jar for up to 3 days.

TO MAKE THE FRIED GREEN TOMATOES

1. Preheat the oven to 425°F. Line a sheet pan with parchment paper. Set aside.

2. In a small bowl, stir together the Parmesan cheese, almond flour, black pepper, garlic powder, paprika, salt, and cayenne. Mix well.

3. In a medium bowl, whisk the almond milk and egg to combine.

4. One at a time, dip the tomato slices into the egg mixture and dredge them in the Parmesan-almond flour mixture, coating both sides well. Place the coated tomato slices on the prepared sheet pan.

5. Bake for about 5 minutes, or until golden brown. Flip the slices over and bake for 5 minutes more. Serve immediately with the avocado ranch.

Time-saving tip: This avocado ranch is dairy-free and so versatile. Make extra and keep it on hand to dress any salad or for dipping veggies.

Nutrition information per serving: Calories: 224; Total Fat: 20g; Protein: 6g; Total Carbs: 5g; Net Carbs: 3g; Fiber: 2g; Sodium: 590mg; Macros: 80% Fat; 11% Protein; 9% Carbs

GRILLED CHICKEN DIABLO BITES

Egg-free, Gluten-free, Nut-free

SERVES 10 / PREP TIME: 20 MINUTES / COOK TIME: 30 MINUTES

These diablos get their name from the double whammy of the spicy pepper Jack cheese and jalapeños nestled inside that juicy bacon-wrapped chicken. These can be made ahead of time so all you have to do is cook, slice, and serve when the party starts. Perfect for game day or tailgating.

6 boneless chicken thighs

Kosher salt

Freshly ground black pepper

Garlic powder, for seasoning

Paprika, for seasoning

½ sweet onion, or purple onion, cut into 4 or 5 wedges

3 jalapeño peppers, halved lengthwise, seeded and ribbed

6 ounces pepper Jack cheese, cut into 6 slices

6 smoked bacon slices

Guacamole, for serving

1. Preheat a grill to 350°F to 400°F or preheat the oven to 400°F. If using the oven, line a sheet pan with parchment paper. Set aside.

2. Place the chicken thighs between two pieces of heavy plastic wrap and, using a meat mallet, pound them out until about ¼ inch thick. Liberally season the chicken on both sides with salt, pepper, garlic powder, and paprika. Season the onion and jalapeños with salt and pepper.

3. Place a chicken thigh, smooth-side down, on a cutting board. In the center of the chicken, place a piece of onion and a piece of pepper Jack cheese. Place a jalapeño half, cut-side down, over the cheese, so it covers the cheese. Fold one end of the chicken thigh tightly over the jalapeño and repeat with the other end. Wrap 1 piece of bacon tightly around the bundle and secure it with a toothpick. Repeat with the remaining chicken thighs.

4. Grill the chicken bundles for 25 to 30 minutes, or until the cheese melts and the chicken is cooked through and the juices run clear. Alternatively, place the chicken bundles on the prepared sheet pan and bake for 25 to 30 minutes, or until the chicken is cooked through and the juices run clear.

5. Cut the chicken bundles into ½- to 1-inch slices and secure with toothpicks, if needed, for serving. Serve warm with guacamole for dipping.

Nutrition information per serving: Calories: 277; Total Fat: 21g; Protein: 21g; Total Carbs: 1g; Net Carbs: 1g; Fiber: 0g; Sodium: 544mg; Macros: 68% Fat; 30% Protein; 2% Carbs

Easy Herbed Tomato Bisque with Onion
Cheddar Grilled Cheese Dippers, page 83

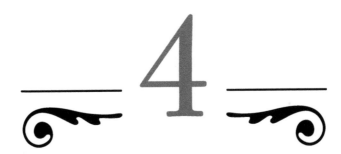

SALADS, SIDES, AND SOUPS

MIMS'S OIL AND VINEGAR COLESLAW

Dairy-free, Egg-free, Gluten-free, Nut-free, Vegan

SERVES 6 / PREP TIME: 20 MINUTES / CHILL TIME: 1 HOUR

Mims is my godfather's mother and my caretaker for the first few years of my life. Some of my earliest childhood memories are with her and her grandkids. She was a great cook and one of my favorite dishes she made was her coleslaw, which, by the way, was no ordinary slaw. The combination of veggies is what makes this recipe special and, for most of my life, it was the only coleslaw I would eat. Over the years I've made a few tweaks to make it keto friendly but I don't think even Mims could tell the difference.

3 cups shredded cabbage

2 (2.5-ounce) cans sliced black olives, drained

1 cup diced green bell pepper

1 cup diced celery

1 cup diced English cucumber

3 tablespoons finely diced purple onion

1 (4-ounce) jar diced pimientos, drained

¼ cup red wine vinegar

1½ teaspoons kosher salt

½ teaspoon onion powder

½ teaspoon dry mustard

½ teaspoon monk fruit/erythritol blend sweetener

¼ teaspoon freshly ground black pepper

¼ teaspoon granulated garlic

⅓ cup light olive oil, or avocado oil

1. In a large bowl, combine the cabbage, olives, green bell pepper, celery, cucumber, onion, and pimientos.

2. In a pint-size jar, combine the vinegar, salt, onion powder, mustard, sweetener, pepper, granulated garlic, and oil. Cover the jar tightly and shake to combine. Pour the dressing over the veggies and toss to coat.

3. Refrigerate for at least 1 hour before serving. The longer it sits, the better it gets.

Nutrition information per serving: Calories: 80; Total Fat: 4g; Protein: 2g; Total Carbs: 9g; Net Carbs: 6g; Fiber: 3g; Sodium: 2360mg; Erythritol Carbs 0g; Macros: 45% Fat; 10% Protein; 45% Carbs

SOUTHERN FRIED CABBAGE

5 Ingredients, Dairy-free, Egg-free, Gluten-free, Nut-free, Vegan

SERVES 6 TO 8 / PREP TIME: 15 MINUTES / COOK TIME: 43 MINUTES

Fried cabbage is one of my family's favorite sides and one we often make into a complete meal by adding sausage or any leftover meat. As the cabbage cooks, it gets a little sweeter and starts to caramelize, which is my favorite part. I do have to say that I've burned cabbage more often in my kitchen than any other food, so keep a close eye on it.

3 tablespoons olive oil, or bacon drippings if you have some on hand

½ cup diced onion

1 large head cabbage, cleaned, cored and diced into 1-inch pieces

1½ teaspoons kosher salt, plus more as needed

1 teaspoon garlic powder

½ teaspoon freshly ground black pepper, plus more as needed

3 tablespoons water (optional)

1. Preheat a large sauté pan or skillet over medium heat. Add the olive oil and onion, and sauté for 2 to 3 minutes.

2. Add the cabbage, salt, garlic powder, and pepper. (The skillet will be very full but the cabbage will wilt while cooking.) Cook, stirring, for about 5 minutes, until the cabbage begins to wilt. Reduce the heat to low and cover the skillet. Cook for 25 to 30 minutes, or until the cabbage is tender. (Note that cabbage has a tendency to burn as it cooks, so cook on low heat and stir often. You may need to add 2 to 3 tablespoons of water to the cabbage as it cooks if you see it starting to brown too soon.)

3. Uncover the skillet and cook for 5 minutes more, stirring often. Don't walk away at this point. Cook the cabbage until it begins to brown and caramelize a bit. Taste and season with more salt and pepper, as needed.

Nutrition information per serving: Calories: 127; Total Fat: 7g; Protein: 3g; Total Carbs: 13g; Net Carbs: 7g; Fiber: 6g; Sodium: 619mg; Macros: 50% Fat; 9% Protein; 41% Carbs

DEVILED EGG SALAD WITH BACON

Dairy-free, Gluten-free, Nut-free

SERVES 6 / PREP TIME: 15 MINUTES / CHILL TIME: 4 HOURS

This easy salad is perfect for meal prep and great to have on hand for
a quick meal when turning on the stove is not an option. Full of texture,
it's perfect served wrapped in lettuce or in an avocado boat,
scooped up with cucumber slices or just straight up.

8 hard-boiled eggs, peeled
and chopped

1 cup diced celery

4 scallions, sliced

¾ cup mayonnaise

2 teaspoon Dijon mustard

¾ teaspoon kosher salt

½ teaspoon hot sauce

½ teaspoon gluten-free
Worcestershire sauce

¼ teaspoon freshly ground
black pepper

¼ teaspoon paprika

¼ teaspoon onion powder

¼ teaspoon garlic powder

8 crispy cooked bacon
slices, chopped

1 tablespoon chopped fresh parsley

1. In a medium bowl, combine the eggs, celery, and scallions. Toss
to combine.

2. In a small bowl, whisk the mayonnaise, mustard, salt, hot sauce, Worcestershire sauce, pepper, paprika, onion powder, and garlic powder. Pour
the mayonnaise mixture over the eggs and gently stir to combine.

3. Stir in the bacon and parsley. Cover and refrigerate for 2 to 4 hours
before serving.

Nutrition information per serving: Calories: 413; Total Fat: 37g; Protein: 17g; Total Carbs: 3g; Net
Carbs: 2g; Fiber: 1g; Sodium: 1188mg; Macros: 81% Fat; 16% Protein; 3% Carbs

CRISP AND CREAMY SOUTHERN COLESLAW

Gluten-free, Nut-free, Vegetarian

SERVES 6 TO 8 / PREP TIME: 10 MINUTES / CHILL TIME: 30 MINUTES

Creamy, tangy, slightly sweet coleslaw is a Southern meal must-have. After the coleslaw is dressed, it can get a little soggy if it sits too long, so I like to use broccoli slaw to help keep it crisp. This creamy coleslaw is perfect paired with Ranch Favorite Texas-Style Pulled Pork (page 146) or any barbecue, fried fish, or chicken.

½ cup mayonnaise

½ cup sour cream

1½ to 2 tablespoons monk fruit/ erythritol blend sweetener

1½ tablespoons apple cider vinegar

1½ teaspoons mustard

½ teaspoon kosher salt

¼ teaspoon freshly ground black pepper

¼ teaspoon paprika

¼ teaspoon onion powder

⅛ teaspoon garlic powder

1 (14-ounce) package shredded cabbage or coleslaw mix

1 (12-ounce) package broccoli slaw

1. In a small bowl, whisk the mayonnaise, sour cream, sweetener, vinegar, mustard, salt, pepper, paprika, onion powder, and garlic powder until smooth and the sweetener is dissolved. Set aside.

2. In a large bowl, combine the cabbage and broccoli slaw. Add the dressing and toss to combine. Refrigerate at least 30 minutes before serving to let the flavors mingle.

Nutrition information per serving: Calories: 206; Total Fat: 18g; Protein: 3g; Total Carbs: 9g; Net Carbs: 5g; Fiber: 4g; Sodium: 355mg; Erythritol Carbs: 2g; Macros: 79% Fat; 4% Protein; 17% Carbs

GREEN CHILE CAULIFLOWER RICE BAKE

Egg-free, Gluten-free, Nut-free, Vegetarian

This creamy, green chile rice dish was always reserved for special occasions and has shown up on our family table time and again. It's one of those dishes I always hoped was on the menu because it's just so good. I took a few liberties with the original recipe to make it keto and, I have to say, I like this version better than the original . . . sorry, mom!

2 tablespoons butter, plus more for preparing the baking dish

2½ cups cooked cauliflower rice

¾ cup chopped celery

½ cup chopped white onion

½ cup heavy (whipping) cream

1 cup shredded Monterey Jack cheese

1 cup shredded sharp Cheddar cheese

1 (4-ounce) can green chilies, drained

½ cup sour cream

1½ teaspoons kosher salt

½ teaspoon freshly ground black pepper

½ teaspoon granulated garlic

1. Preheat the oven to 325°F. Coat an 8-by-8-inch baking dish with butter. Set aside.

2. Place the cooked cauliflower rice between paper towels and squeeze it to remove any excess moisture. Set aside. You want the rice to be fairly dry so your dish isn't watery.

3. In a sauté pan or skillet over medium-high heat, melt the butter. Add the celery and onion. Cook for 5 to 7 minutes, or until tender.

4. Reduce the heat to medium and stir in the heavy cream. Cook for 3 to 4 minutes, stirring constantly, until the mixture is reduced by half, and thick and creamy. Set aside.

5. In a large bowl, combine the cauliflower rice, ½ cup of Monterey Jack cheese, ½ cup of Cheddar cheese, the green chilies, sour cream, vegetable-cream mixture, salt, pepper, and granulated garlic. Stir to combine. Spread the mixture evenly in the prepared pan and top with the remaining ½ cup of Monterey Jack and Cheddar cheeses.

6. Bake for 20 to 25 minutes, or until bubbly.

Variation tip: Add leftover shredded chicken to the cauliflower mixture before baking to create an easy, delicious dinner the whole family will go crazy for.

Nutrition information per serving: Calories: 328; Total Fat: 28g; Protein: 12g; Total Carbs: 7g; Net Carbs: 5g; Fiber: 2g; Sodium: 901mg; Macros: 77% Fat; 15% Protein; 8% Carbs

CHEESY "HASH BROWN" CASSEROLE

Egg-free, Gluten-free, Nut-free

SERVES 8 / PREP TIME: 15 MINUTES / COOK TIME: 50 MINUTES

Every Southern family has a name for this comforting casserole. Sometimes called "funeral potatoes" or just "hash brown casserole," you'll often find this cheesy dish served at church gatherings, potlucks, and family holidays. This keto version uses shredded turnips in place of the traditional potatoes to keep the carb count at a minimum. You'll want to use medium or small turnips, as the larger ones tend to be more bitter.

Nonstick cooking spray

2 pounds turnips, peeled and shredded

1¾ teaspoons kosher salt, divided

4 tablespoons butter

⅓ cup diced onion

¼ cup chicken stock

1 cup heavy (whipping) cream

¾ cup sour cream

¼ teaspoon freshly ground black pepper

¼ teaspoon garlic powder

2 cups shredded Cheddar cheese, divided

2 scallions, sliced

1. Preheat the oven to 350°F. Coat an 8-by-8-inch baking dish with cooking spray. Set aside.

2. In a medium bowl, toss together the turnips and 1 teaspoon of salt. Let sit for 10 minutes.

3. Meanwhile, in a sauté pan or skillet over medium heat, melt the butter. Add the onion and sauté for 5 to 7 minutes, or until the onion is translucent but not brown.

4. Add the chicken stock to the onion and simmer for 1 to 2 minutes. Add the heavy cream and simmer for 5 to 7 minutes until the mixture is reduced and thick. Remove from the heat.

5. Place the turnips between two paper towels, or wrap them in a clean kitchen towel, and squeeze to remove any excess liquid. Place the squeezed turnips in a bowl. Add the sour cream, the remaining ¾ teaspoon of salt, the pepper, garlic powder, onion mixture, and 1½ cups of Cheddar cheese. Mix until thoroughly combined. Pour the mixture into the prepared baking dish and cover with aluminum foil.

6. Bake for 35 minutes. Remove from the oven, top with the remaining ½ cup of Cheddar cheese, and bake for 10 more minutes. Garnish with scallions and serve warm.

Nutrition information per serving: Calories: 359; Total Fat: 31g; Protein: 10g; Total Carbs: 10g; Net Carbs: 7g; Fiber: 3g; Sodium: 825mg; Macros: 78% Fat; 11% Protein; 11% Carbs

CREAMY MASHED "FAUXTATOS"

Egg-free, Gluten-free, Nut-free, Vegetarian

SERVES 6 / PREP TIME: 15 MINUTES / COOK TIME: 25 MINUTES

Missing your mashed potatoes? These creamy, dreamy mashed turnips are my favorite low-carb potato alternative. Turnips have an earthiness that offers so much more flavor than traditional potatoes.

1½ pounds (about 6) turnips, peeled and diced

2 teaspoons kosher salt

3 ounces cream cheese

5 tablespoons butter

3 tablespoons heavy (whipping) cream

Kosher salt

Freshly ground black pepper

Chopped scallion, or fresh chives, for garnish

1. Fill a large pot with about 8 cups of cold water. Add the turnips and salt. Place the pot over high heat and bring to a boil. Reduce the heat to maintain a simmer and cook the turnips for 15 to 20 minutes, until tender. Drain the turnips and return them to the pot. Return the pot to the burner but leave the burner off and let the turnips sit for 1 to 2 minutes so some of the excess moisture evaporates.

2. Remove the pot from the burner. Add the cream cheese, butter, and heavy cream. Mash until your desired consistency is reached. Taste and season with salt and pepper, as needed.

Variation tip: Make it a loaded "fauxtato" bake! Stir 3 tablespoons sour cream into the prepared mashed turnips and pour them into a small casserole dish. Top with shredded cheese and crumbled bacon. Bake at 350°F for 10 to 12 minutes until the cheese is melted and the dish is warmed through. Top with chives.

Troubleshooting tip: Large turnips tend to be bitter, so stick to turnips that are about baseball size for the best flavor. If you do get a larger turnip that's a little bitter, add ½ to 1 teaspoon sweetener to the water before boiling.

Nutrition information per serving: Calories: 202; Total Fat: 18g; Protein: 2g; Total Carbs: 8g; Net Carbs: 6g; Fiber: 2g; Sodium: 575mg; Macros: 80% Fat; 4% Protein; 16% Carbs

STEWED OKRA WITH TOMATOES AND BACON

Dairy-free, Egg-free, Gluten-free, Nut-free

SERVES 6 TO 8 / PREP TIME: 15 MINUTES / COOK TIME: 35 MINUTES

Okra and tomatoes go together like two peas in a pod, and bacon just takes it over the top. This simple stewed okra dish is one my mom has been making for years and is still one of my favorites. The addition of the acidic tomatoes helps cut down on okra's undesirable (sometime slimy) textural issues.

8 thick-cut bacon slices, diced

½ cup diced onion

⅓ cup diced red bell pepper

2 garlic cloves, finely minced

4 cups fresh okra, sliced

3 tomatoes, diced

½ teaspoon kosher salt

½ teaspoon freshly ground black pepper

1 tablespoon chopped fresh parsley

1. In a large, deep sauté pan or skillet over medium heat, cook the bacon for 7 to 10 minutes until crispy. Using a slotted spoon, transfer the bacon to paper towels to drain, leaving the fat in the skillet.

2. Return the skillet to the heat. Add the onion and red bell pepper to the bacon drippings and sauté for 3 to 5 minutes, until the onion is translucent.

3. Add the garlic and cook for 1 to 2 minutes more.

4. Add the okra, tomatoes, salt, and pepper. Cover the skillet and simmer for 20 to 25 minutes, stirring occasionally, or until the okra is tender.

5. Sprinkle the bacon and parsley over the okra before serving.

Variation tip: To spice things up a bit, reduce the fresh tomato by one and add one can of diced tomatoes with green chilies.

Nutrition information per serving: Calories: 244; Total Fat: 16g; Protein: 16g; Total Carbs: 9g; Net Carbs: 6g; Fiber: 3g; Sodium: 1080mg; Macros: 60% Fat; 20% Protein; 20% Carbs

MOM'S CORN BREAD DRESSING

Gluten-free

SERVES 9 / PREP TIME: 15 MINUTES / COOK TIME: 45 MINUTES

**My mom is famous, at least in our family, for her corn bread dressing.
In fact, she has to triple her recipe to keep up with holiday demand
for leftovers. This recipe has all the goodness of my mom's corn bread
dressing—ketofied! You will have to taste the dressing a few times to adjust
the seasoning, especially if you're using pan juices instead of stock.**

1 recipe Sour Cream Corn Bread (page 15)

2 tablespoons butter, plus more for preparing the baking dish

1 cup diced celery

½ cup diced green bell pepper

½ cup diced onion

1 teaspoon kosher salt, plus more as needed

1 teaspoon poultry seasoning, plus more as needed

½ teaspoon garlic powder

½ teaspoon freshly ground black pepper, plus more as needed

1½ teaspoons dried parsley

1½ cups pan juices and drippings from a cooked turkey, or chicken stock

1 egg, beaten

1. Preheat the oven to 250°F. Line a sheet pan with parchment paper.

2. Crumble the corn bread onto the prepared sheet pan.

3. Bake for 10 to 15 minutes to slightly dry out the bread. Set aside to cool.

4. Increase the oven temperature to 350°F. Coat a medium casserole dish with butter. Set aside.

5. In a medium sauté pan or skillet over medium heat, melt the butter. Add the celery, green bell pepper, onion, salt, poultry seasoning, garlic powder, and pepper. Cook for about 7 to 10 minutes until the onion is translucent and the vegetables are tender.

6. In a large bowl, combine the crumbled corn bread, parsley, and cooked vegetables. Stir to combine. Taste and add more poultry seasoning or salt.

7. Add the pan juices and gently stir to moisten the corn bread. Taste and add more salt and pepper, as needed.

8. Add the egg and stir to incorporate fully. Pour the stuffing mixture into the prepared dish.

9. Bake for 20 to 25 minutes, or until golden brown on top. Serve warm.

Variation tip: Feel free to change this up to fit your family's tastes. Sausage and sage stuffing? Add 8 ounces cooked sausage to the dressing mix before baking. Don't like bell pepper? Use mushrooms. Vegetarian? Use vegetable broth.

Nutrition information per serving: Calories: 209; Total Fat: 17g; Protein: 7g; Total Carbs: 7g; Net Carbs: 3g; Fiber: 4g; Sodium: 526mg; Erythritol Carbs: 0g; Macros: 74% Fat; 13% Protein; 13% Carbs

ASPARAGUS AND SPINACH CASSEROLE WITH MUSHROOMS AND FONTINA

Egg-free, Gluten-free, Vegetarian

SERVES 9 / PREP TIME: 15 MINUTES / COOK TIME: 45 MINUTES

This vegetable casserole is a twist on my favorite spinach Parmesan side dish. For this version, I've added asparagus, hearty mushrooms, and creamy Fontina cheese to create a sauce that will have you licking your plate. This casserole is perfect served next to simple roasted chicken or a grilled steak.

4 tablespoons butter, plus more for preparing the baking dish

8 ounces cremini mushrooms, cleaned and sliced

½ cup diced onion

½ teaspoon kosher salt

2 garlic cloves, finely minced

¼ teaspoon freshly ground black pepper

¾ cups heavy (whipping) cream

½ cup unsweetened almond milk

2 ounces cream cheese, at room temperature

1¾ cups shredded Fontina cheese

¾ cup grated Parmesan cheese, divided

1 pound fresh asparagus, woody ends trimmed, cut into 1½-inch pieces

2 (10-ounce) packages frozen chopped spinach, thawed and squeezed dry

1. Preheat the oven to 350°F. Coat a 9-by-9-inch baking dish with butter. Set aside.

2. In a medium sauté pan or skillet over medium heat, melt the butter. Add the mushrooms, onion, and salt. Sauté for 5 to 7 minutes, or until the onion is translucent and the mushrooms have started to brown.

3. Add the garlic and cook for 1 minute more.

4. Stir in the heavy cream, almond milk, and cream cheese, stirring until the cream cheese is completely melted. Simmer for 5 minutes, stirring often.

5. Remove the skillet from the heat and stir in the Fontina cheese and ½ cup of Parmesan cheese, stirring until the cheese is fully incorporated. Set aside.

6. In a large bowl, combine the asparagus and spinach. Pour the cream mixture into the bowl and stir well to combine. Pour the mixture into the prepared baking dish and top with the remaining ¼ cup of Parmesan cheese.

7. Bake for 25 to 30 minutes, or until golden brown and bubbly. Let cool for 5 minutes before serving.

How-to tip: The ends of asparagus can be extremely tough and fibrous, so you want to be sure to trim them. To trim the asparagus, hold the end of the spear with one hand, with the other hand around the middle of the spear. Bend the spear until it snaps and discard the woody end.

Nutrition information per serving: Calories: 300; Total Fat: 24g; Protein: 13g; Total Carbs: 8g; Net Carbs: 5g; Fiber: 3g; Sodium: 508mg; Macros: 72% Fat; 17% Protein; 11% Carbs

MAPLE PECAN BRUSSELS SPROUTS WITH BACON

Egg-free, Gluten-free

SERVES 8 / PREP TIME: 15 MINUTES / COOK TIME: 25 MINUTES

My family adores Brussels sprouts—and this maple, bacon, pecan combo is a winner. The slightly sweet notes from the maple syrup are a perfect match for the salty bacon and rich pecans. Blanching the sprouts ahead helps ensure they cook quickly once in the pan.

Kosher salt

2 pounds fresh Brussels sprouts, trimmed and cleaned

6 bacon slices, diced

2 tablespoons finely diced purple onion

Freshly ground black pepper

¾ cup heavy (whipping) cream

1 tablespoon sugar-free maple syrup

¼ chopped pecans, toasted

1. Fill a large stockpot with water, add a few good pinches of salt, and place the pot over high heat to bring to a boil.

2. Add the Brussels sprouts. Cook for 4 to 5 minutes . . . no more! Drain the sprouts and place them in a bowl of ice water for about 2 minutes to stop the cooking. Remove the sprouts from the ice bath and transfer to a few layers of paper towels to dry. Once dry, halve the sprouts and set aside.

3. In a large sauté pan or skillet over medium heat, cook the bacon for 7 to 10 minutes until crisp and golden brown. Using a slotted spoon, remove the bacon from the skillet, leaving the fat in the pan. Reserve the crispy bacon.

4. Return the skillet to the heat, add the purple onion, and cook for 1 to 2 minutes. Add the sprouts, 1½ teaspoons of salt, and ½ teaspoon of pepper. Increase the heat to medium-high. Cook the sprouts for 5 to 7 minutes until they are tender and begin to brown and caramelize.

5. Stir in the heavy cream and syrup. Cook for 2 to 3 minutes, or until the cream is reduced and the sauce thickens. Taste and add more salt and pepper, as needed.

6. Sprinkle with toasted pecans and reserved bacon, and serve warm.

Time-saving tip: Blanch and prepare the sprouts the day before your meal (steps 1 and 2). Refrigerate in a zip-top bag until needed.

Nutrition information per serving: Calories: 258; Total Fat: 18g; Protein: 11g; Total Carbs: 13g; Net Carbs: 8g; Fiber: 5g; Sodium: 386mg; Macros: 63% Fat; 17% Protein; 20% Carbs

SWEET "FAUXTATO" CASSEROLE

....

Gluten-free, Vegetarian

SERVES 9 / PREP TIME: 20 MINUTES / COOK TIME: 1 HOUR

In most Southern kitchens, sweet potatoes are a constant. Unfortunately, they have too many carbs to be keto friendly but, with a few swaps, you can make a Sweet "Fauxtato" Casserole that will satisfy your sweet potato cravings. I used roasted acorn squash in this casserole for the flavor and texture, and add a little pumpkin to round out everything. I'll tell you a little secret . . . I'm not a lover of sweet potatoes but this imposter casserole is so good I find myself eating it right from the pan!

....

1 acorn squash, quartered and seeded

Oil, for roasting and preparing the baking dish

1 teaspoon kosher salt

⅓ cup pumpkin purée

5 tablespoons monk fruit/erythritol blend sweetener

4 tablespoons butter, melted

¼ cup heavy (whipping) cream

1½ teaspoons ground cinnamon

1 teaspoon vanilla extract

1 egg, beaten

⅓ cup chopped pecans

1. Preheat the oven to 375°F. Line a sheet pan with parchment. Lightly coat an 8-by-8-inch baking dish with oil and set aside.

2. Place the squash on the prepared sheet pan, drizzle with oil, and lightly season with salt.

3. Roast for 25 to 35 minutes, or until the squash is fork-tender. Set aside to cool.

4. Reduce the oven temperature to 350°F.

5. Once the squash is cool, remove the peel and place the flesh into a large bowl. Using a fork, mash the squash, leaving a few lumps here and there.

6. Add the pumpkin, sweetener, butter, heavy cream, cinnamon, salt, vanilla, and egg. Mix well to combine, breaking up the squash as needed. Pour the mixture into the prepared baking dish and spread it evenly. Top with the pecans.

7. Bake for 20 to 25 minutes. Keep an eye on the casserole to make sure the nuts don't burn. If needed, cover the baking dish loosely with aluminum foil. Serve warm.

Allergen tip: For a lactose-free version, replace the butter with ghee and substitute coconut cream for the heavy cream. Bake as directed.

Nutrition information per serving: Calories: 144; Total Fat: 12g; Protein: 2g; Total Carbs: 7g; Net Carbs: 5g; Fiber: 2g; Sodium: 307mg; Erythritol Carbs: 7g; Macros: 75% Fat; 6% Protein; 19% Carbs

ROASTED POBLANO CAULIFLOWER "MAC" AND CHEESE

Egg-free, Gluten-free, Nut-free, Vegetarian

SERVES 6 / PREP TIME: 10 MINUTES / COOK TIME: 25 MINUTES

I grew up eating cauliflower "mac" and cheese and just never knew it! My mom would often serve cauliflower covered in cheese sauce. This version dresses up the cauliflower with flavorful roasted poblanos and, paired with creamy Monterey Jack cheese, it has become a family favorite . . . even for those who aren't keto.

Nonstick cooking spray

6 cups cauliflower florets

¾ cup heavy (whipping) cream

3 ounces cream cheese

½ teaspoon kosher salt

¼ teaspoon onion powder

¼ teaspoon garlic powder

¼ teaspoon paprika

¼ teaspoon freshly ground black pepper

1¼ cups shredded Monterey Jack cheese

2 poblano peppers, roasted and chopped (see How-to tip)

1. Preheat the oven to 350°F. Lightly coat a 9-by-9-inch baking dish with cooking spray. Set aside.

2. In a large microwave-safe bowl, combine the cauliflower and ¼ cup water. Cover and microwave for 6 to 7 minutes, or until just tender. Transfer the cauliflower to paper towels to absorb some of the moisture. Discard the cooking liquid left in the bowl. Return the cauliflower to the bowl and set aside.

3. In a saucepan over medium heat, combine the heavy cream, cream cheese, salt, onion powder, garlic powder, paprika, and pepper. Bring the mixture to a boil. Reduce the heat to maintain a simmer and cook for 1 to 2 minutes. Remove the cream mixture from the heat and stir in 1 cup of Monterey Jack cheese, stirring until the cheese is fully melted. Stir in the roasted poblanos.

4. Pour the cheese sauce over the cauliflower and gently toss to combine. Pour the cauliflower into the prepared baking dish. Top with the remaining ¼ cup of Monterey Jack cheese.

5. Bake for 10 to 15 minutes, or until bubbly and golden.

How-to tip: To roast the poblanos, preheat the oven to 450°F. Line a sheet pan with parchment paper and place the poblanos on the prepared pan. Drizzle lightly with oil. Roast for 10 to 12 minutes, turning once, until the skins are blistered and charred. Transfer the peppers to a paper bag or a glass bowl. Tightly fold down the bag or cover the bowl with plastic wrap and set the peppers aside to cool. Once cooled, remove the stems, seeds, and skins from the peppers.

Nutrition information per serving: Calories: 279; Total Fat: 23g; Protein: 10g; Total Carbs: 8g; Net Carbs: 5g; Fiber: 3g; Sodium: 404mg; Macros: 74% Fat; 14% Protein; 12% Carbs

CHICKEN TACO SOUP WITH CAULIFLOWER RICE

Dairy-free, Egg-free, Gluten-free, Nut-free

SERVES 6 TO 8 / PREP TIME: 30 MINUTES / COOK TIME: 30 MINUTES

There's nothing like the comforting aromas of a big pot of chicken soup simmering on the stove, and it seems every Southerner I know has their own version. My version is spiced with warm, south-of-the-border flavors and is completely dairy-free.

¼ cup avocado oil

¾ cup diced celery with leaves

½ cup diced onion

1½ teaspoons kosher salt, divided

3 garlic cloves, minced

1 cup diced zucchini

2 tablespoons chili powder

1 tablespoon dried parsley

1¼ teaspoons granulated garlic

1¼ teaspoons ground cumin

1¼ teaspoons paprika

½ teaspoon freshly ground black pepper

½ teaspoon dried Mexican oregano

6 cups chicken stock or bone broth

3 cups shredded cooked chicken thighs

2 (12-ounce) packages frozen cauliflower rice

Chopped fresh cilantro, for garnish

Diced avocado, for garnish

1. In a large stockpot over medium heat, heat the avocado oil. Add the celery, onion, and ½ teaspoon of salt. Sauté for about 5 minutes, or until tender.

2. Add the garlic cloves, zucchini, chili powder, parsley, granulated garlic, cumin, paprika, remaining 1 teaspoon of salt, the pepper, and oregano. Cook for 1 to 2 minutes more, stirring constantly.

3. Stir in the chicken stock. Bring the mixture to boil and reduce the heat to maintain a simmer. Simmer, uncovered, for 10 to 15 minutes.

4. Add the chicken and cauliflower rice. Simmer the soup for 10 minutes more, or until the veggies are tender. Serve warm topped with cilantro and avocado.

....

Time-saving tip: To get this hearty dinner on the table in a snap, use deboned leftover chicken or rotisserie chicken.

Nutrition information per serving: Calories: 262; Total Fat: 14g; Protein: 24g; Total Carbs: 10g; Net Carbs: 5g; Fiber: 5g; Sodium: 1480mg; Macros: 48% Fat; 37% Protein; 15% Carbs

LOADED BAKED "FAUXTATO" SOUP

Egg-free, Gluten-free, Nut-free

SERVES 6 / PREP TIME: 15 MINUTES / COOK TIME: 20 MINUTES

This Loaded Baked "Fauxtato" Soup will warm your keto soul when the temperatures dip down. It's simple to make and is so luscious you won't want to put down your spoon.

3 tablespoons butter

1¼ pounds turnips (about 5), peeled and diced into 1-inch cubes

¼ cup chopped onion

1 teaspoon kosher salt, plus more as needed

½ teaspoon garlic powder

12 ounces cauliflower florets, fresh or frozen, steamed until just tender

2½ to 3 cups chicken stock, plus more as needed

⅓ cup heavy (whipping) cream

2 tablespoons sour cream

Freshly ground black pepper

Crispy, chopped cooked bacon, for garnish

Shredded Cheddar cheese, for garnish

Sliced scallion, for garnish

1. In a medium saucepan over medium heat, melt the butter. Add the turnips, onion, salt, and garlic powder. Sauté for 8 to 10 minutes until the onion is tender and the turnips begin to pick up some golden brown color. Add the cauliflower and cook for 1 to 2 minutes more.

2. Add the chicken stock and bring the mixture to a boil. Lower the heat to maintain a simmer and cook for 7 to 8 minutes, or until the turnips are fork-tender. Remove from the heat and let cool a few minutes.

3. Carefully pour the soup into a blender. Add the heavy cream and sour cream. Blend on high speed until smooth and creamy. Adjust the consistency with additional broth, and adjust the seasoning, as needed.

4. Serve topped with bacon, cheese, and scallion.

Nutrition information per serving: Calories: 324; Total Fat: 24g; Protein: 14g; Total Carbs: 13g; Net Carbs: 9g; Fiber: 4g; Sodium: 939mg; Macros: 67% Fat; 17% Protein; 16% Carbs

EASY HERBED TOMATO BISQUE WITH ONION CHEDDAR GRILLED CHEESE DIPPERS

Gluten-free

SERVES 8 / PREP TIME: 15 MINUTES / COOK TIME: 25 MINUTES

Just the thought of warm tomato soup and grilled cheese brings a smile to my face. This flavorful tomato bisque is so easy, creamy, and delicious— and served with Onion Cheddar Grilled Cheese Dippers, to die for!

3 tablespoons olive oil

½ cup diced onion

2 garlic cloves, roughly chopped

1 (28-ounce) can whole tomatoes (San Marzano style are best)

1 cup chicken stock or bone broth

1 tablespoon tomato paste

½ teaspoon dried basil

½ teaspoon dried thyme

1 tablespoon freshly squeezed lemon juice

½ cup heavy (whipping) cream

1 recipe Onion Cheddar Grilled Cheese Dippers (see Onion Cheddar Bread, Variation tip, page 24)

1. In a Dutch oven over medium heat, combine the olive oil and onion. Sauté for about 5 minutes until the onion is translucent, but not brown. Add the garlic and cook for 1 minute more.

2. Stir in the tomatoes, chicken stock, tomato paste, basil, and thyme, stirring to break up the chunks of tomato. Reduce the heat to low and simmer the soup for 15 to 20 minutes. Carefully transfer the soup to a blender and blend until smooth. Use caution while blending hot liquids and cover the lid with a towel. Pour the soup back into the pan and stir in the lemon juice and heavy cream.

3. Serve hot with Onion Cheddar Grilled Cheese Dippers for, well, dipping.

Nutrition information per serving (½ cup): Calories: 358; Total Fat: 30g; Protein: 10g; Total Carbs: 12g; Net Carbs: 6g; Fiber: 6g; Sodium: 416mg; Macros: 75% Fat; 12% Protein; 13% Carbs

Oven-Baked Chiles Rellenos
with Avocado Crema, page 88

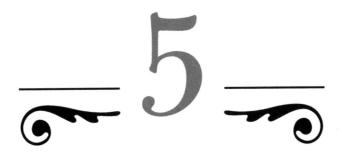

VEGETARIAN MAINS

ROASTED SQUASH AND TOMATO PIE

Gluten-free, Vegetarian

SERVES 8 / PREP TIME: 30 MINUTES / COOK TIME: 1 HOUR, 10 MINUTES

A spin on the Southern classic tomato pie, this keto version has roasted squash, which not only turns up the flavor but helps lower the carb count by replacing some of the tomatoes. This pie is best eaten the day it's made and is ideal for using up those summer garden veggies.

FOR THE PIE FILLING

2 zucchini, cut into ¼-inch-thick slices

1 yellow squash, cut into ¼-inch-thick slices

3 tablespoons olive oil

¾ teaspoon kosher salt, divided

½ teaspoon freshly ground black pepper, divided

2 cups shredded mozzarella cheese, divided

¼ cup grated Parmesan cheese

¼ cup mayonnaise

1 egg

¼ teaspoon minced garlic

¼ teaspoon dried basil

1 ripe tomato, cut into ¼-inch-thick slices

FOR THE PIE CRUST

3 ½ tablespoons butter, melted, plus more for preparing the pie pan

1½ cups almond flour

¼ cup grated Parmesan cheese

¼ teaspoon freshly ground black pepper

¼ teaspoon garlic powder

Pinch kosher salt

TO START THE PIE FILLING

1. Preheat the oven to 400°F. Line a sheet pan with parchment paper. Set aside.

2. In a large bowl, toss together the zucchini, squash, olive oil, ½ teaspoon of salt, and ¼ teaspoon of pepper. Spread the vegetables on the prepared sheet pan.

3. Roast for 20 to 25 minutes, flipping the vegetables halfway through the cooking time, until tender and beginning to caramelize. Set aside to cool.

4. Lower the oven temperature to 350°F.

TO MAKE THE PIE CRUST

1. Coat a 9-inch pie pan with butter. Set aside.

2. In a small bowl, stir together the almond flour, Parmesan cheese, pepper, garlic powder, and salt. Pour in the melted butter and stir until thoroughly incorporated. The mixture will be crumbly. Firmly press the crust mixture evenly into the bottom and up the sides of the prepared pie pan.

3. Bake for 12 to 14 minutes, or until the edges are golden brown. Leave the oven on.

TO FINISH THE PIE FILLING

1. While the crust bakes, in a medium bowl, stir together 1¾ cups of mozzarella cheese, the Parmesan cheese, mayonnaise, egg, garlic, basil, and the remaining ¼ teaspoon each of salt and pepper.

2. Layer half the roasted squash in the bottom of the piecrust. Spread half the mozzarella cheese mixture over the top. Top the cheese mixture with the tomato slices. Evenly spread the remaining squash over the tomatoes and top with the remaining mozzarella cheese mixture and remaining ¼ cup of mozzarella cheese.

3. Bake for 25 to 30 minutes, or until the top is golden brown and the edges are bubbly. Let the pie cool for 20 to 30 minutes before slicing. Best served warm or at room temperature.

Nutrition information per serving: Calories: 346; Total Fat: 30g; Protein: 13g; Total Carbs: 6g; Net Carbs: 4g; Fiber: 2g; Sodium: 558mg; Macros: 78% Fat; 15% Protein; 7% Carbs

OVEN-BAKED CHILES RELLENOS WITH AVOCADO CREMA

Egg-free, Gluten-free, Nut-free, Vegetarian

SERVES 6 / PREP TIME: 35 MINUTES / COOK TIME: 10 MINUTES

When I have company, I love to serve stuffed peppers. Not only are they delicious but they give the impression I've put a ton of effort into the preparation of dinner (which really couldn't be easier). Traditionally, *chiles rellenos* are battered and fried but this oven-baked version highlights the flavor of the poblano pepper. These gorgeous chiles rellenos are stuffed with Mexican cauliflower rice and gooey cheese for a hearty filling and topped with an easy avocado *crema*.

FOR THE AVOCADO CREMA

1 cup sour cream

¼ avocado

¼ cup fresh cilantro

1 garlic clove, peeled

1 tablespoon heavy (whipping) cream or half-and-half

½ teaspoon kosher salt

FOR THE CHILES RELLENOS

4 large or 6 medium poblano peppers, washed

2 tablespoons avocado oil, olive oil, or ghee

½ cup diced onion

½ cup diced green bell pepper

2 garlic cloves, finely minced

1½ teaspoons chili powder

½ teaspoon ground cumin

2 (12-ounce) packages frozen cauliflower rice

1½ teaspoons kosher salt

½ teaspoon garlic powder

1½ cups shredded Monterey Jack cheese, divided

TO MAKE THE AVOCADO CREMA

In a blender, combine the sour cream, avocado, cilantro, garlic, heavy cream, and salt. Blend until smooth. Transfer the crema to a bowl and refrigerate until needed.

TO MAKE THE CHILES RELLENOS

1. Preheat the oven to 425°F. Line a sheet pan with parchment paper.

2. Place the poblanos on the prepared sheet pan and roast for about 20 minutes, or until the skins are blistered. Remove from the oven to cool. Cut a slit down the peppers lengthwise, and remove the stem and seeds. Place the peppers back on the sheet pan.

3. Preheat a sauté pan or skillet over medium heat. Add the avocado oil, onion, and green bell pepper. Sauté for 3 to 5 minutes, or until the onion is translucent. Stir in the garlic, chili powder, and cumin. Sauté for 1 minute more, stirring constantly.

4. Stir in the cauliflower rice, salt, and garlic powder. Cook for 7 to 10 minutes, stirring often, until the cauliflower rice is cooked and there is no liquid left in the pan.

5. Stir in 1 cup of Monterey Jack cheese. Divide the cauliflower rice mixture among the 6 peppers, stuffing the cavities and mounding the filling. I do this right on the sheet pan.

6. Top the peppers with the remaining ½ cup of Monterey Jack cheese.

7. Bake for 10 minutes, or until the cheese is melted and bubbly. Serve warm topped with the avocado crema.

Allergen tip: To make these chiles rellenos dairy-free, omit the cheese from the filling and serve with guacamole instead of the avocado crema.

Nutrition information per serving: Calories: 299; Total Fat: 23g; Protein: 11g; Total Carbs: 12g; Net Carbs: 7g; Fiber: 5g; Sodium: 921mg; Macros: 70% Fat; 15% Protein; 15% Carbs

CRUSTLESS CREAM CHEESE AND SPINACH QUICHE

Gluten-free, Nut-free, Vegetarian

SERVES 8 / PREP TIME: 15 MINUTES / COOK TIME: 35 MINUTES

Frozen spinach is a versatile and nutritious vegetable I love to keep stocked. Quick and easy, this delicious spinach quiche is perfect for meal prep.

3 tablespoons butter, plus more for preparing the pie pan

¼ cup chopped onion

2 garlic cloves, finely chopped

4 eggs, lightly beaten

4 ounces cream cheese, at room temperature

⅓ cup whole-milk ricotta

¾ teaspoon kosher salt

¼ teaspoon freshly ground black pepper

10 ounces frozen chopped spinach, thawed and squeezed dry

3 tablespoons diced roasted red pepper

¼ cup shredded Parmesan cheese

1. Preheat the oven to 350°F. Coat a 9-inch pie pan with butter. Set aside.

2. In a small sauté pan or skillet over medium heat, melt the butter. Add the onion and garlic, and sauté for about 5 minutes until tender. Set aside.

3. In a large bowl, whisk the eggs, cream cheese, ricotta, salt, and pepper.

4. Stir in the onions and garlic, spinach, and roasted red pepper and mix well to combine. Pour the mixture into the prepared pie pan and top with the Parmesan cheese.

5. Bake for about 30 minutes, or until set. Let cool for 15 to 20 minutes before slicing. Best served warm or at room temperature.

How-to tip: Once thawed, frozen spinach has excess moisture you don't want in your gorgeous quiche. It will make it soggy. To dry your spinach, first squeeze it over a colander. Then press it between paper towels to remove any excess moisture.

Nutrition information per serving: Calories: 166; Total Fat: 14g; Protein: 7g; Total Carbs: 3g; Net Carbs: 2g; Fiber: 1g; Sodium: 401mg; Macros: 76% Fat; 17% Protein; 7% Carbs

COLLARD GREENS AND RICOTTA-STUFFED PORTOBELLOS

Egg-free, Gluten-free, Nut-free, Vegetarian

SERVES 4 / PREP TIME: 15 MINUTES / COOK TIME: 22 MINUTES

Collard greens are traditional in the South and often, on Sunday, you'd find a batch cooking away on the stovetop. They're fairly mild and often sweeter than other greens and are delicious as a stuffing for portobello mushrooms.

4 medium portobello mushrooms, stemmed and gills removed

2 tablespoons avocado oil

½ teaspoon kosher salt

3 tablespoons butter

½ cup diced onion

2 garlic cloves, finely chopped

2 cups frozen collard greens

½ cup whole-milk ricotta

½ cup shredded mozzarella cheese

¼ cup grated Parmesan cheese

¼ teaspoon freshly ground black pepper

⅛ teaspoon garlic powder

1. Preheat the oven to 400°F. Line a sheet pan with parchment paper.

2. Place the portobellos, gill-side up, on the prepared sheet pan. Brush them with olive oil and sprinkle lightly with salt.

3. Roast for 10 to 12 minutes. Set aside.

4. Meanwhile, in a medium sauté pan over medium heat, melt the butter. Add the onion and garlic. Sauté for about 5 minutes until translucent. Add the collards and cook for 5 to 7 minutes until tender. Set aside to cool.

5. In a large bowl, stir together the ricotta, mozzarella and Parmesan cheeses, pepper, and garlic powder. Stir in the cooled collard greens. Evenly divide the mixture among the portobellos.

6. Bake for 7 to 10 minutes, or until golden brown and bubbly. Let sit 5 minutes before serving.

Nutrition information per serving: Calories: 282; Total Fat: 22g; Protein: 12g; Total Carbs: 9g; Net Carbs: 5g; Fiber: 4g; Sodium: 528mg; Macros: 70% Fat; 17% Protein; 13% Carbs

ROASTED BROCCOLI STEAKS WITH PIMIENTO CHEESE BUTTER

Egg-free, Gluten-free, Nut-free, Vegetarian

SERVES 6 / PREP TIME: 10 MINUTES / COOK TIME: 30 MINUTES

I love roasting my vegetables, and if you haven't tried roasted broccoli yet, bless your heart—you're missing out! These broccoli steaks are roasted until tender and slightly browned and caramelized, then topped with a flavor-packed Southern-inspired pimiento cheese butter. It's broccoli and cheese on a whole 'nother level!

Olive oil

3 large broccoli crowns, halved through the stem ends

Kosher salt

½ cup shredded medium Cheddar cheese or Colby cheese

4 tablespoons butter, at room temperature

¼ cup mayonnaise

1 (4-ounce) jar diced pimientos, drained

¼ teaspoon garlic powder

⅛ teaspoon freshly ground black pepper

1. Preheat the oven to 375°F. Line a sheet pan with parchment paper, brush the parchment with olive oil, and set aside.

2. Brush the broccoli crowns all over with olive oil and season with salt. Place them on the prepared sheet pan, cut-side down.

3. Roast for 20 to 25 minutes, or until just tender.

4. In a small bowl, stir together the Cheddar cheese, butter, mayonnaise, pimientos, garlic powder, and pepper.

5. Evenly divide the pimiento cheese butter among the broccoli crowns. Bake for 5 minutes more, or until the cheese is melted and bubbly. Serve warm.

Nutrition information per serving: Calories: 283; Total Fat: 23g; Protein: 7g; Total Carbs: 12g; Net Carbs: 7g; Fiber: 5g; Sodium: 236mg; Macros: 73% Fat; 10% Protein; 17% Carbs

CREAMY ZUCCHINI GRUYÈRE CASSEROLE

Gluten-free, Nut-free, Vegetarian

SERVES 8 / PREP TIME: 15 MINUTES / COOK TIME: 40 MINUTES

This casserole features a velvety Gruyère custard that's delicious paired with zucchini. To avoid excess liquid in the casserole, the zucchini is sautéed first. Serve with a simple salad for an elegant and easy vegetarian meal.

3 tablespoons butter, plus more for preparing the pie pan

4 zucchini, cut into ¼-inch-thick slices

½ chopped onion

1 teaspoon kosher salt, divided

¼ teaspoon freshly ground black pepper

3 eggs

1 cup shredded Gruyère cheese

½ cup heavy (whipping) cream

¼ cup plus 2 tablespoons grated Parmesan cheese, divided

1 teaspoon gluten-free Worcestershire Sauce

¼ teaspoon dried basil

1. Preheat the oven to 350°F. Coat a 9-inch pie pan with butter. Set aside.

2. In a large sauté pan or skillet over medium-high heat, melt the butter. Add the zucchini, onion, salt, and pepper. Sauté for 7 to 10 minutes until tender, stirring occasionally. Spread the cooked zucchini evenly over the bottom of the prepared pie pan and set aside.

3. In a large bowl, whisk the eggs, Gruyère cheese, heavy cream, ¼ cup of Parmesan cheese, the remaining ½ teaspoon of salt, and Worcestershire sauce until smooth. Stir in the basil. Pour the mixture evenly over the zucchini and top with remaining 2 tablespoons of Parmesan cheese.

4. Bake for 25 to 30 minutes, or until set. Let cool 20 to 30 minutes before slicing. Best served warm or at room temperature.

Nutrition information per serving: Calories: 209; Total Fat: 17g; Protein: 9g; Total Carbs: 5g; Net Carbs: 3g; Fiber: 2g; Sodium: 442mg; Macros: 73% Fat; 17% Protein; 10% Carbs

PORTOBELLO AND EGGPLANT SHEET PAN FAJITAS

Dairy-free, Egg-free, Gluten-free, Nut-free, Vegan

SERVES 5 / PREP TIME: 15 MINUTES / COOK TIME: 25 MINUTES

I love eggplant, especially roasted. Caramelized on the exterior and creamy and luxurious on the inside, it's perfect paired with meaty portobello mushrooms, zucchini, and sweet peppers for these easy sheet pan fajitas. My family loves these served with steamed cauliflower rice and topped with all our favorite toppings—salsa, guacamole, cheese, sour cream— and finished with a squeeze of fresh lime juice.

1 red bell pepper, seeded and cut into strips

1 green bell pepper, seeded and cut into strips

2 zucchini, cut into ½-inch matchsticks

2 portobello mushrooms, cleaned and cut into ½-inch slices

1 poblano pepper, seeded and cut into thin strips

1 eggplant, peeled and cut into ½-inch matchsticks

½ purple onion, sliced

¼ cup avocado oil

2½ teaspoons chili powder

2 teaspoons kosher salt

1½ teaspoons garlic powder

1 teaspoon freshly ground black pepper

1 teaspoon paprika

1 teaspoon ground cumin

Steamed cauliflower rice, for serving

Sour cream, for garnish

Shredded cheese, for garnish

Salsa, for garnish

Guacamole, for garnish

Chopped fresh cilantro, for garnish

Lime wedges, for squeezing

1. Preheat the oven to 425°F. Line a large sheet pan with parchment paper. Set aside.

2. In a large bowl, combine the red and green bell peppers, zucchini, mushrooms, poblano, eggplant, and onion. Set side.

3. In a small bowl, whisk the avocado oil, chili powder, salt, garlic powder, pepper, paprika, and cumin until blended. Pour the seasoned oil over the veggies and toss to coat. Pour the veggies onto the prepared sheet pan and spread them into a single layer.

4. Roast for 20 to 25 minutes until tender and slightly charred, stirring occasionally. Serve over steamed cauliflower rice, garnished as desired.

Time-saving tip: I always have frozen cauliflower rice on hand to serve with quick weeknight meals like these fajitas.

Nutrition information per serving: Calories: 280; Total Fat: 20g; Protein: 8g; Total Carbs: 17g; Net Carbs: 10g; Fiber: 7g; Sodium: 939mg; Macros: 65% Fat; 11% Protein; 24% Carbs

VEGETARIAN STUFFED CORN BREAD CASSEROLE

Gluten-free, Vegetarian

SERVES 8 / PREP TIME: 15 MINUTES / COOK TIME: 45 MINUTES

Stuffed corn bread casserole is always a hit during the colder months. This flavor-packed version is stuffed with a chili-inspired vegetable filling. Topped with cheese and a keto-friendly corn bread topping, this casserole will satisfy the meat lovers in the family, too.

FOR THE VEGETABLE FILLING

3 tablespoons avocado oil, plus more for preparing the pie pan

2 zucchini, diced

8 ounces mushrooms, diced

1 eggplant, peeled and diced

1 poblano pepper, diced

½ cup diced onion

⅓ cup diced green bell pepper

1½ teaspoons kosher salt, plus more as needed

2 garlic cloves, finely diced

2 teaspoons chili powder

1 teaspoon paprika

1½ cups water or vegetable stock

1 tablespoon tomato paste

Freshly ground black pepper

1 cup shredded Monterey Jack or Colby cheese

FOR THE CORN BREAD TOPPING

1 cup almond flour

2½ tablespoons coconut flour

2½ teaspoons baking powder

½ teaspoon kosher salt

¼ teaspoon garlic powder

¼ teaspoon onion powder

4 eggs, lightly beaten

5 tablespoons butter, melted

2 tablespoons sour cream

TO MAKE THE VEGETABLE FILLING

1. Coat a 9-inch deep-dish pie pan or baking dish with avocado oil. Set aside.

2. In a large Dutch oven over medium-high heat, combine the avocado oil, zucchini, mushrooms, eggplant, poblano, onion, green bell pepper, and salt. Reduce the heat to medium and cook for 8 to 10 minutes until the vegetables are tender.

3. Stir in the garlic, chili powder, and paprika. Cook for 1 to 2 minutes more.

4. Stir in the water and tomato paste. Simmer the filling for 5 to 7 minutes, or until thickened. Taste and add more salt and pepper, as needed. Pour the filling into the prepared pie pan. Set aside.

TO MAKE THE CORN BREAD TOPPING

1. Preheat the oven to 350°F.

2. In a large bowl, stir together the almond and coconut flours, baking powder, salt, garlic powder, and onion powder.

3. Add the eggs, melted butter, and sour cream. Stir well to combine.

4. Sprinkle the Monterey Jack cheese evenly over the vegetable filling.

5. Pour the batter over the cheese, spreading it to the edges of the pan to seal in the filling.

6. Bake for about 25 minutes, or until the topping is golden brown.

Nutrition information per serving: Calories: 329; Total Fat: 25g; Protein: 12g; Total Carbs: 14g; Net Carbs: 7g; Fiber:7g; Sodium: 776mg; Macros: 68% Fat; 15% Protein; 17% Carbs

SPINACH ARTICHOKE POTPIE

Gluten-free, Vegetarian

SERVES 9 / PREP TIME: 20 MINUTES / COOK TIME: 32 MINUTES

This dreamy potpie was inspired by my love of warm spinach artichoke dip. If this decadent and addictive dip was served at a gathering or party, you could find me camped out next to the appetizer table. This potpie showcases everything that makes the classic so delicious and is topped with a buttery keto drop biscuit topping that will knock your socks off!

FOR THE PIE FILLING

2 tablespoons butter, plus more for preparing the baking dish

2 (10-ounce) packages frozen chopped spinach, thawed and drained well

⅓ cup finely diced onion

1 garlic clove, finely chopped

1 (14-ounce) can artichoke hearts, drained and roughly chopped

6 ounces cream cheese, at room temperature

¾ cup grated Parmesan cheese

¼ cup sour cream

¼ cup mayonnaise

2 tablespoons diced pimiento

¾ teaspoon kosher salt

¼ teaspoon freshly ground black pepper

¼ teaspoon gluten-free Worcestershire sauce

Pinch cayenne pepper

FOR THE BISCUIT TOPPING

1½ cups almond flour

2½ tablespoons coconut flour

1 tablespoon baking powder

1½ teaspoons monk fruit/erythritol blend sweetener

½ teaspoon kosher salt

2 eggs

2 tablespoons sour cream

5 tablespoons butter

TO MAKE THE PIE FILLING

1. Preheat the oven to 350°F. Lightly coat an 8-by-8-inch baking dish with butter. Set aside.

2. Press the spinach between paper towels to remove any excess liquid. Set aside.

3. In a sauté pan or skillet over medium heat, melt the butter. Add the onion and garlic. Sauté for 5 to 7 minutes until the onion is translucent. Transfer to a large bowl and add the spinach, chopped artichokes, cream cheese, Parmesan cheese, sour cream, mayonnaise, pimiento, salt, black pepper, Worcestershire sauce, and cayenne. Stir well to combine and pour the filling into the prepared baking dish. Set aside.

TO MAKE THE BISCUIT TOPPING

1. In a medium bowl, stir together the almond and coconut flours, baking powder, sweetener, and salt.

2. Add the eggs and sour cream, and stir to combine.

3. Pour in the melted butter and stir until fully incorporated. Drop the biscuit dough by scant ¼-cup dollops onto the filling.

4. Bake for about 25 minutes, or until golden brown.

Nutrition information per serving: Calories: 368; Total Fat: 28g; Protein: 13g; Total Carbs: 16g; Net Carbs: 8g; Fiber: 8g; Sodium: 691mg; Erythritol Carbs: 0g; Macros: 68% Fat; 14% Protein; 18% Carbs

SPAGHETTI SQUASH CASSEROLE

Egg-free, Gluten-free, Nut-free, Vegetarian

SERVES 8 / PREP TIME: 20 MINUTES / COOK TIME: 1 HOUR, 30 MINUTES

Spaghetti squash takes a little prep work but is worth it in the end. Great as a substitute for pasta, this delicious squash is a little higher in carbs than other squash, like zucchini, so it's important to watch portion sizes. That said, this squash is versatile and can be used to add variety to your keto recipe arsenal. This casserole can be served as a main dish with a simple salad or as a side to a larger meal.

Olive oil

1 spaghetti squash (about 3 pounds)

¼ teaspoon kosher salt, plus more for seasoning

¼ teaspoon freshly ground black pepper, plus more for seasoning

2 tablespoons butter

½ cup diced onion

2 garlic cloves, finely chopped

½ cup heavy (whipping) cream

½ cup feta cheese

2 ounces cream cheese, at room temperature

¼ cup sliced scallion

1½ teaspoons chopped fresh parsley

½ teaspoon granulated garlic

1 egg, lightly beaten

⅓ cup grated Parmesan cheese

1. Preheat the oven to 400°F. Line a sheet pan with parchment paper. Set aside. Coat a 9-by-9-inch baking dish with olive oil. Set aside.

2. Pierce the squash several times with a fork. Microwave the whole squash for 5 to 7 minutes to soften it slightly. Be careful when removing the squash, as the skin will be hot. Trim off both ends of the squash and cut the squash lengthwise down the middle. Scrape out and discard the seeds. Drizzle the cut sides of the squash with olive oil and season lightly with salt and pepper. Place the squash, cut-side down, on the prepared sheet pan.

3. Roast for 40 to 45 minutes, or until fork-tender. Set aside to cool slightly. Using a fork, scrape across the squash surface to create spaghetti-like strands. Transfer the strands to a large bowl.

4. Reduce the oven temperature to 350°F.

5. In large sauté pan or skillet over medium-high heat, melt the butter. Add the onion and cook for about 5 minutes, or until softened. Add the garlic and cook for 1 minute more. Transfer the veggies to a medium bowl and let cool.

6. To the vegetable mixture, add the heavy cream, feta cheese, cream cheese, scallion, parsley, granulated garlic, salt, and pepper. Stir to combine. Add to the cooked spaghetti squash and toss to mix.

7. Stir in the egg and pour the mixture into the prepared baking dish. Top with the Parmesan cheese.

8. Bake for 25 to 30 minutes, or until set. Serve warm.

How-to tip: When selecting a spaghetti squash, look for one that's firm, heavy, and free of any spots, cracks, or soft spots. You also want the squash to have a dry stem free of any moisture. Spaghetti squash can be stored up to 1 month in a cool, dry space.

Nutrition information per serving: Calories: 225; Total Fat: 17g; Protein: 6g; Total Carbs: 12g; Net Carbs: 10g; Fiber: 2g; Sodium: 312mg; Macros: 68% Fat; 11% Protein; 21% Carbs

Sheet Pan Seafood Boil, page 106

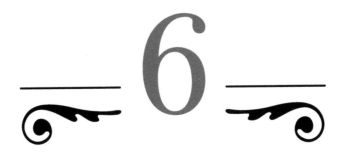

FISH AND SEAFOOD

CREAMY SHRIMP AND GRITS CASSEROLE

Gluten-free

SERVES 6 / PREP TIME: 15 MINUTES / COOK TIME: 40 MINUTES

My mom makes a shrimp and grits casserole that's so good, it'll bring a tear to your eye. What better inspiration for my ketofied version?

FOR THE GRITS

3 tablespoons butter, plus more for preparing the baking dish

½ teaspoon minced garlic

¾ cup almond flour

1½ tablespoons coconut flour

¾ cup almond milk

3 tablespoons heavy (whipping) cream

¼ teaspoon kosher salt

⅛ teaspoon freshly ground black pepper

½ cup shredded Cheddar cheese

1 egg, lightly beaten

FOR THE SHRIMP

6 thick-cut bacon slices, diced

½ cup diced onion

⅓ cup diced green bell pepper

2 garlic cloves, finely chopped

¼ cup white wine

¼ cup chicken stock or bone broth

1 teaspoon dried parsley

½ teaspoon dried thyme

½ teaspoon kosher salt

½ teaspoon freshly ground black pepper

⅛ teaspoon cayenne pepper

1½ pounds medium raw shrimp, peeled and deveined

¾ cup heavy (whipping) cream

3 scallions, sliced

TO MAKE THE GRITS

1. Preheat the oven to 350°F. Coat an 8-inch square baking dish with butter. Set aside.

2. In a medium saucepan over medium heat, melt the butter. Add the garlic and sauté for 1 to 2 minutes.

3. Stir in the almond and coconut flours.

4. Add the almond milk, heavy cream, salt, and pepper. Bring the mixture to a simmer. Cook, stirring constantly, for 2 to 3 minutes until thickened. Remove from the heat and stir in the Cheddar cheese.

5. Whisk the egg into the mixture and pour the grits into the prepared baking dish.

6. Bake for 12 to 15 minutes, or until golden around the edges and set in the center.

TO MAKE THE SHRIMP

1. In a large sauté pan or skillet over medium-high heat, cook the bacon for 7 to 10 minutes until crispy. Using a slotted spoon, transfer the bacon to paper towels to drain, leaving the fat in the skillet.

2. Return the skillet to the heat and add the onion and green bell pepper to the bacon drippings. Sauté for 3 to 5 minutes until softened. Add the garlic and cook for 1 minute more, stirring constantly.

3. Add the wine and chicken stock. Simmer for 3 to 4 minutes until reduced by about half.

4. Add the parsley, thyme, salt, black pepper, and cayenne. Cook for 1 to 2 minutes more.

5. Add the shrimp and heavy cream. Simmer for 3 to 5 minutes until the sauce is thickened and the shrimp are cooked through and opaque. Pour the shrimp mixture over the baked grits. Garnish with scallions and reserved crispy bacon. Serve immediately.

Nutrition information per serving: Calories: 581; Total Fat: 45g; Protein: 34g; Total Carbs: 10g; Net Carbs: 5g; Fiber: 5g; Sodium: 1364mg; Macros: 70% Fat; 23% Protein; 7% Carbs

SHEET PAN SEAFOOD BOIL

Egg-free, Gluten-free, Nut-free

SERVES 6 / PREP TIME: 15 MINUTES / COOK TIME: 35 MINUTES

When we have large groups of guests out on the ranch, we often do a seafood boil, and everyone goes crazy for it! Typically, we do our big boils on the propane burner outside or in the barn, but when it's just the family, this sheet pan version is the perfect size and can be done in the oven in no time flat. We love the combination of shrimp, mussels, clams, sausage, and veggies, but this meal can be customized to fit the likes of your family or guests. We take the sheet pan to the table and eat family style with some butter on the side for dipping.

1½ pounds turnips, peeled and cut into ½-inch pieces

Kosher salt

¾ cup (1½ sticks) butter, melted, plus more for serving

1½ tablespoons Old Bay seasoning

1½ tablespoon freshly squeezed lemon juice

1 tablespoon minced garlic

1 teaspoon gluten-free Worcestershire sauce

2 pounds medium raw shrimp, rinsed

1 pound mussels or clams, cleaned (frozen will work as well)

1 pound andouille sausage or kielbasa, cut into 2-inch pieces

1 pound asparagus, woody ends trimmed

1 small onion, peeled and cut into 8 wedges

Lemon wedges, for serving

1. Preheat the oven to 475°F. Line 2 large sheet pans with parchment paper. Set aside.

2. In a medium saucepan, combine the turnips, a pinch of salt, and enough water to cover. Place the pan over high heat and bring to a boil. Cook for 12 to 15 minutes, or until fork-tender. Drain and set aside.

3. In a small bowl, stir together the melted butter, Old Bay seasoning, lemon juice, garlic, and Worcestershire sauce. Set aside.

4. Evenly divide the shrimp, mussels, sausage, cooked turnips, asparagus, and onion between the prepared sheet pans. Drizzle half the butter mixture over each sheet pan. Toss the seafood and vegetables with the butter to coat. Tightly cover each pan with aluminum foil.

5. Bake for 15 to 20 minutes, or until the shrimp are pink and done, and the shellfish are opened. Discard any shellfish that have not opened. Serve family style with fresh lemon wedges for squeezing and melted butter for dipping.

Nutrition information per serving: Calories: 588; Total Fat: 40g; Protein: 42g; Total Carbs: 15g; Net Carbs: 10g; Fiber: 5g; Sodium: 2346mg; Macros: 61% Fat; 29% Protein; 10% Carbs

SHRIMP AND ANDOUILLE JAMBALAYA

Egg-free, Gluten-free, Nut-free

SERVES 6 / PREP TIME: 15 MINUTES / COOK TIME: 30 MINUTES

If you're on the hunt for a quick and easy weeknight comfort food dish, look no further! This Cajun-inspired dinner uses frozen cauliflower rice and comes together in a flash. Traditionally, jambalaya is made with white rice, which adds a creamy texture to the dish. Here we add a little cream to finish this rice-free version and mimic that luxurious feel.

1 pound andouille sausage, cut into ¼- to ½-inch slices, then cut into half-moons

1 cup diced celery

1 cup diced green bell pepper

½ cup diced onion

½ teaspoon kosher salt

3 garlic cloves, finely chopped

2 (12-ounce) packages frozen cauliflower rice

1 (15-ounce) can diced tomatoes

2 teaspoons Old Bay seasoning

½ teaspoon dried thyme

½ teaspoon paprika

1½ pounds medium raw shrimp, peeled and deveined

¼ cup heavy (whipping) cream

¼ cup sliced scallion

2 tablespoons chopped fresh parsley

1. Preheat a large sauté pan or skillet over medium-high heat. Add the sausage and cook for about 4 minutes until golden. Using a slotted spoon, remove the sausage, leaving the drippings in the skillet.

2. Return the skillet to the heat and add the celery, green bell pepper, onion, and salt to the drippings. Cook for 5 to 7 minutes, or until the vegetables are tender.

3. Add the garlic and frozen cauliflower rice. Cook, stirring constantly, for 3 to 4 minutes until there is no liquid in the pan.

4. Lower the heat to medium and stir in the tomatoes, Old Bay seasoning, thyme, paprika, and cooked sausage. Cook for 2 to 3 minutes, stirring often, until the liquid is reduced. Add the shrimp and cook for 5 minutes more until the shrimp are pink and opaque.

5. Stir in the heavy cream. Garnish with scallion and parsley for serving.

Allergen tip: This hearty dish can easily be made dairy-free by omitting the cream.

Nutrition information per serving: Calories: 455; Total Fat: 27g; Protein: 38g; Total Carbs: 15g; Net Carbs: 10g; Fiber: 5g; Sodium: 2067mg; Macros: 55% Fat; 33% Protein; 12% Carbs

SEARED BROWN BUTTER SCALLOPS WITH CREAMY CAULIFLOWER RICE

Egg-free, Gluten-free

SERVES 6 / PREP TIME: 15 MINUTES / COOK TIME: 20 MINUTES

We're seafood lovers around here and scallops are definitely one of our favorite treats. Believe it or not, crispy, pan-seared scallops are easy to cook at home and paired with browned butter—incredibly delicious. The secret to perfectly seared scallops is that they must be very dry and your pan needs to be hot. They take just minutes to cook so have your creamy cauliflower rice ready to go before you drop them in the pan.

FOR THE CAULIFLOWER RICE

- 2 (10- to 12-ounce) packages frozen cauliflower rice, cooked according to the package directions, cooled
- 2 tablespoons butter
- ¼ cup diced onion
- 1 garlic clove, finely minced
- ¾ cup heavy (whipping) cream
- ¼ cup unsweetened almond milk (not vanilla)
- ¼ cup grated Parmesan cheese
- ½ teaspoon dried parsley
- Kosher salt
- Freshly ground black pepper

FOR THE SCALLOPS

- 18 ounces sea scallops, at room temperature
- 4 tablespoons butter

TO MAKE THE CAULIFLOWER RICE

1. Press the cooled cauliflower rice between paper towels to remove excess moisture. Set side.

2. In a large sauté pan or skillet over medium heat, melt the butter. Add the onion and cook for 3 to 4 minutes until translucent but not browned. Add the garlic and cook for 1 minute more.

3. Stir in the heavy cream and almond milk. Cook for 1 to 2 minutes, reducing slightly until thickened. Remove from the heat and stir in the Parmesan cheese and parsley.

4. Stir in the cauliflower rice. Season with salt and pepper. Keep warm.

TO MAKE THE SCALLOPS

1. Place the raw scallops on a few paper towels and press them down and pat both sides dry. You need the scallops to be very dry, so don't rush this. When they are dry enough they will stick to the paper towel. Lightly season both sides with salt and pepper.

2. In a large heavy-bottomed skillet or cast-iron pan over medium-high heat, melt the butter. Cook the butter for 1 to 2 minutes, stirring often, until it just starts to turn golden.

3. Add the scallops to the pan in a single layer without touching. Sear for about 2 minutes per side, or until golden brown, basting occasionally with the browned butter. Remove the scallops from the pan. Serve immediately over the creamy cauliflower rice and drizzle with the browned butter.

How-to tip: When selecting scallops, they should have a slightly sweet odor and very little liquid. Sand often accumulates in the crevices of scallops, so rinse them well before cooking. If purchasing scallops in advance, store them loosely covered in the coldest part of the refrigerator and cook within 2 days.

Nutrition information per serving: Calories: 316; Total Fat: 24g; Protein: 18g; Total Carbs: 7g; Net Carbs: 5g; Fiber: 2g; Sodium: 325mg; Macros: 68% Fat; 23% Protein; 9% Carbs

SHRIMP VERACRUZ

Dairy-free, Egg-free, Gluten-free, Nut-free

SERVES 6 / PREP TIME: 10 MINUTES / COOK TIME: 15 MINUTES

My husband loves fishing at the coast and often tries to make it to the docks in the morning, before heading home, to get fresh Gulf shrimp right off the boat. When he gets home, we cook it as a special treat for dinner and this recipe is a definite favorite. This one-pan meal may have simple ingredients, but the flavors are out of this world! Fresh and bright with spicy, south-of-the-border flair.

1½ pounds shrimp, peeled and deveined

Kosher salt

Freshly ground black pepper

Garlic powder, for seasoning

Chili powder, for seasoning

3 tablespoons ghee or avocado oil, divided

½ cup diced onion

½ cup diced green bell pepper

4 garlic cloves, finely minced

3 large ripe tomatoes, seeded and diced

1 tablespoon finely diced jalapeño pepper

½ teaspoon ground cumin

½ cup water or chicken stock

Chopped fresh cilantro, for garnish

Sliced scallion, for garnish

Steamed cauliflower rice or zucchini noodles, for serving

Lime wedges, for serving

1. Pat the shrimp dry with paper towels and lightly season both sides with salt, pepper, garlic powder, and chili powder.

2. Preheat a large heavy skillet or cast-iron pan over medium-high heat. Add 2 tablespoons of ghee to melt.

3. Add the shrimp and cook for about 2 minutes per side until golden brown. Remove from the skillet and set aside.

4. Return the skillet to the heat and add the remaining 1 tablespoon of ghee, the onion, and green bell pepper. Sauté for 2 to 3 minutes until the onion is translucent, scraping up any browned bits from the bottom of the pan.

5. Add the garlic, tomatoes, jalapeño, ½ teaspoon of salt, ¼ teaspoon of garlic powder, and the cumin. Cook for 1 to 2 minutes more, stirring constantly.

6. Add the water to the skillet and simmer for about 3 minutes until the sauce has thickened.

7. Add the shrimp to the pan and cook for 2 minutes more, just until the shrimp are cooked and heated through.

8. Garnish with cilantro and scallion. Serve over cauliflower rice with lime wedges for squeezing.

How-to tip: To seed fresh, ripe tomatoes easily, cut off the stem end of the tomato and halve the tomato lengthwise. Using a spoon, scrape out the seeds and juice (and discard), leaving only the tomato flesh. Dice or chop as desired.

Nutrition information per serving: Calories: 221; Total Fat: 9g; Protein: 25g; Total Carbs: 10g; Net Carbs: 6g; Fiber: 4g; Sodium: 187mg; Macros: 37% Fat; 45% Protein; 18% Carbs

EASY OVEN-FRIED CATFISH

Dairy-free, Gluten-free

SERVES 4 / PREP TIME: 10 MINUTES / SOAK TIME: 3 HOURS
TO OVERNIGHT / COOK TIME: 30 MINUTES

It goes without saying, Southerners and Texans love their fried catfish.
I consider my husband a connoisseur of fried catfish—he knows his stuff
because his granny taught him well and passed on her secrets. Catfish has a
tendency to taste a little muddy, so soaking it in a mixture of water and baking
soda was Granny's solution to that problem and her secret to incredibly tasty
catfish. She used cornmeal to bread her fish, but we're using a blend of almond
flour and pork rinds to create a crispy crust that would make her proud.

4 catfish fillets

2 teaspoons baking soda

Avocado oil

½ cup almond flour

¼ cup crushed pork rinds

¼ teaspoon paprika

¼ teaspoon garlic powder

¼ teaspoon kosher salt

⅛ teaspoon cayenne pepper

2 eggs, lightly beaten

1. Place the catfish in a large bowl of cold water, add the baking soda,
    and stir to combine. Let the fish soak in the refrigerator for a few hours
    to overnight.

2. Preheat the oven to 350°F. Line a sheet pan with parchment paper and
    brush it liberally with avocado oil. Set aside.

3. Drain the catfish, rinse it, and pat it dry with a paper towel.

4. In a shallow pie plate, stir together the almond flour, pork rinds, paprika,
    garlic powder, salt, and cayenne. In another shallow dish, whisk the
    beaten eggs and 1 tablespoon water to combine.

5. Coat each catfish fillet in the egg mixture and dredge it in the almond flour mixture, coating both sides well. Place the fillets, not touching, on the prepared sheet pan.

6. Bake for 25 to 30 minutes, or until the fish is cooked through and flaky, turning the fish halfway through the baking time. Serve with Spicy Tartar Sauce (see Crab Cakes with Spicy Tartar Sauce, page 118).

Nutrition information per serving: Calories: 308; Total Fat: 20g; Protein: 30g; Total Carbs: 2g; Net Carbs: 1g; Fiber: 1g; Sodium: 946mg; Macros: 60% Fat; 36% Protein; 4% Carbs

SHEET PAN SALMON WITH LEMON GREEN BEANS

Egg-free, Gluten-free, Nut-free

SERVES 4 / PREP TIME: 10 MINUTES / COOK TIME: 25 MINUTES

A sheet pan meal is the perfect solution for a busy weeknight, but this gorgeous salmon dinner is even great for entertaining. Salmon is rich in omega-3 fatty acids, potassium, and B vitamins, and is a great source of protein for the keto lifestyle. Fresh green beans are cooked alongside the salmon for a delicious and effortless dinner that can be on the table in about 30 minutes.

3 tablespoons butter

3 garlic cloves, finely chopped

1½ tablespoons freshly squeezed lemon juice

¾ teaspoon kosher salt, plus more for seasoning

½ teaspoon paprika

½ teaspoon garlic powder

¼ teaspoon onion powder

1 pound salmon fillet, or 4 (4-ounce) salmon fillets

12 ounces fresh green beans, trimmed

2 tablespoons olive oil

Freshly ground black pepper

Lemon wedges, for serving

1. Preheat the oven to 400°F. Line a sheet pan with parchment paper. Set aside.

2. In a small microwave-safe bowl, combine the butter, garlic, lemon juice, salt, paprika, garlic powder, and onion powder. Microwave for 30 to 45 seconds until the butter melts. Brush the skin side of the salmon with the butter mixture and place the fish, skin-side down, on the prepared sheet pan. Brush the butter mixture on the other side of the fish.

3. In a medium bowl, toss together the green beans and olive oil. Season with salt and pepper. Spread the green beans in a single layer on the sheet pan around the salmon.

4. Bake for 12 minutes. Flip the salmon over and stir the green beans. Bake for 10 minutes more, or until the salmon is cooked to your desired doneness. Cooking time will depend on the thickness of your fillet.

5. To crisp the skin, broil the salmon for 2 to 3 minutes before removing it from the oven. Serve immediately with lemon wedges for squeezing.

Variation tip: This salmon dish is also great paired with asparagus when it peaks in the spring. Just snap off the tough ends of the asparagus and treat it just like the green beans.

Nutrition information per serving: Calories: 408; Total Fat: 32g; Protein: 21g; Total Carbs: 9g; Net Carbs: 5g; Fiber: 4g; Sodium: 560mg; Macros: 71% Fat; 21% Protein; 8% Carbs

CRAB CAKES WITH SPICY TARTAR SAUCE

Gluten-free, Nut-free

SERVES 8 / PREP TIME: 15 MINUTES / COOK TIME: 25 MINUTES

Crab cakes used to be my go-to at any great seafood restaurant—but not anymore. Now I make amazing, flavorful, keto-friendly crab cakes at home in just a few minutes. Don't forget to make the spicy tartar sauce—it takes these crab cakes over the top!

FOR THE SPICY TARTAR SAUCE

½ cup mayonnaise

1 small garlic clove, grated

2 teaspoons whole-grain mustard

1½ teaspoons freshly squeezed lemon juice

1 teaspoon dill relish

½ teaspoon gluten-free Worcestershire Sauce

¼ teaspoon paprika

¼ teaspoon kosher salt

2 or 3 dashes hot sauce

⅛ teaspoon cayenne pepper

FOR THE CRAB CAKES

3 tablespoons mayonnaise

1 tablespoon freshly squeezed lemon juice

1 tablespoon whole-grain mustard

1½ teaspoons Old Bay seasoning

1 teaspoon gluten-free Worcestershire sauce

¼ teaspoon freshly ground black pepper

2 or 3 dashes hot sauce

Pinch kosher salt

1 pound lump crabmeat

3 tablespoons sliced scallion

2 tablespoons chopped fresh parsley

1 egg, lightly beaten

3½ tablespoons coconut flour

4 tablespoons butter, divided

Lemon wedges, for serving

TO MAKE THE SPICY TARTAR SAUCE

In a small bowl, stir together the mayonnaise, garlic, mustard, lemon juice, relish, Worcestershire sauce, paprika, salt, and hot sauce. Add cayenne to taste and stir to combine. Refrigerate while preparing the crab cakes.

TO MAKE THE CRAB CAKES

1. In a medium bowl, stir together the mayonnaise, lemon juice, mustard, Old Bay seasoning, Worcestershire sauce, black pepper, hot sauce, and salt.

2. Add the crab, scallion, and parsley, and gently toss to coat in the mayonnaise mixture. Gently stir in the egg and coconut flour. Let rest for 5 minutes. Divide the crab mixture into 8 portions and form each into a patty about ½ inch thick.

3. In a large sauté pan or skillet over medium heat, melt 2 tablespoons of butter. Place 2 or 3 crab cakes in the pan and cook for 3 to 4 minutes per side, or until golden. Repeat with the remaining patties.

4. Serve with lemon wedges for squeezing and spicy tartar sauce.

Troubleshooting tip: The best crab cakes barely hold together because they're all luscious crab with little binder. These crab cakes use a little coconut flour and an egg to help bind them together. For easy flipping in the skillet, use a fish turner or thin spatula and don't crowd the skillet with too many crab cakes at once.

Nutrition information per serving: Calories: 219; Total Fat: 15g; Protein: 11g; Total Carbs: 10g; Net Carbs: 6g; Fiber: 4g; Sodium: 642mg; Macros: 62% Fat; 20% Protein; 18% Carbs

BLACKENED REDFISH WITH SPICY CRAWFISH CREAM SAUCE

Less than 30 Minutes, Egg-free, Gluten-free, Nut-free

SERVES 4 / PREP TIME: 10 MINUTES / COOK TIME: 20 MINUTES

Redfish, or red drum, is a popular fish in the South and one my husband often comes home with in the cooler from his trips to the coast. Our favorite way to prepare redfish is to blacken it—it's easy and delicious. The fish is coated in a spice mixture and cooked at a high temperature, so it turns dark and crusts the outside of the fish. It'll cause a little smoke in the kitchen so turn on your vent. Serve this flavor-packed fish on a bed of zucchini noodles and top with this creamy crawfish sauce for a real Cajun-inspired treat. This would also be great with salmon or flounder.

FOR THE BLACKENED REDFISH

1 tablespoon paprika

2 teaspoons kosher salt

1 teaspoon onion powder

1 teaspoon garlic powder

1 teaspoon freshly ground black pepper

½ teaspoon dried thyme

½ teaspoon dried oregano

¼ teaspoon cayenne pepper

4 (4-ounce) redfish fillets, skinned and boned

2 tablespoons butter plus 3 tablespoons butter, melted, divided

FOR THE CREAM SAUCE

2 tablespoons butter

¼ cup sliced scallion

2 garlic cloves, finely minced

⅓ cup chicken broth

2 tablespoons white wine

1 cup heavy (whipping) cream

1 pound crawfish tails, thawed if frozen

XANTHAN GUM
BLACKENED SEASONING

TO MAKE THE BLACKENED REDFISH

1. In a small bowl, stir together the paprika, salt, onion powder, garlic powder, black pepper, thyme, oregano, and cayenne. Set aside.

2. Place the fillets on paper towels and pat dry. Place the 3 tablespoons melted butter in a shallow dish. Dredge each fillet in the melted butter, coating each side well. Liberally sprinkle both sides of the fillets with the blackening seasoning. Reserve ½ teaspoon of seasoning.

3. Turn on your overhead vent. Preheat a large heavy skillet or cast-iron pan over medium- to medium-high heat for 2 to 3 minutes. Add the remaining 2 tablespoons of butter to the pan to melt.

4. Quickly add the fillets to the hot pan and sear for 2 to 3 minutes per side, or until done. To check for doneness, gently pierce the thickest part of the fish with a fork; the fish should flake easily and will be opaque all the way through. Remove the fillets from the pan.

TO MAKE THE CREAM SAUCE

1. Return the skillet to the heat and reduce the heat to medium. Add the butter, scallion, garlic, and reserved ½ teaspoon of seasoning. Sauté for 1 to 2 minutes.

2. Add the chicken broth and wine. Cook for 3 to 4 minutes until reduced by half, stirring constantly to pick up the browned bits left on the bottom of the pan.

3. Add the heavy cream and simmer the sauce for 3 to 4 minutes, stirring constantly until thickened.

4. Add the crawfish tails and stir until heated through. Serve the sauce over the blackened fillets.

Time-saving tip: Use your favorite blackening seasoning instead of making your own. We make a double or triple batch of this seasoning to keep on hand for seasoning anything from chicken to steak and even salmon.

Nutrition information per serving: Calories: 670; Total Fat: 46g; Protein: 58g; Total Carbs: 6g; Net Carbs: 5g; Fiber: 1g; Sodium: 1540mg; Macros: 62% Fat; 35% Protein; 3% Carbs

PECAN-CRUSTED CATFISH

Dairy-free, Gluten-free

SERVES 4 / PREP TIME: 20 MINUTES / COOK TIME: 25 MINUTES

This irresistible pecan-crusted catfish proves there's more than one way to cook mouthwatering, delectable catfish! A rich, savory, and crunchy coating is the perfect match for meaty, moist catfish fillets. Serve this easy fish dish with some Southern Fried Cabbage (page 61) or Stewed Okra with Tomatoes and Bacon (page 69) for a winner, winner catfish dinner!

4 (4-ounce) catfish fillets, rinsed and patted dry

2 cups chopped pecans

1½ teaspoons gluten-free Worcestershire sauce

1¼ teaspoons garlic powder

1¼ teaspoons paprika

1 teaspoon kosher salt, plus more for seasoning

½ teaspoon freshly ground black pepper, plus more for seasoning

¼ teaspoon onion powder

¼ teaspoon cayenne pepper (optional)

2 eggs, lightly beaten

1 teaspoon hot sauce

Chopped fresh parsley, for serving

Lemon wedges, for serving

1. Preheat the oven to 375°F. Line a large sheet pan with parchment paper. Set aside.

2. In a food processor, combine the pecans, Worcestershire sauce, garlic powder, paprika, salt, black pepper, onion powder, and cayenne. Pulse until the pecans are finely chopped. Pour the mixture into a shallow pie plate and set aside.

3. In a separate shallow dish, whisk the eggs and hot sauce.

4. Dip each catfish fillet into the egg, coating it on both sides, and dredge in the pecan mixture, pressing the pecan coating onto the fish as needed to make sure the top of the fillet is well coated. Place the fillets onto the prepared baking sheet.

5. Bake for 20 to 25 minutes, or until done and the pecan crust is golden brown and fragrant. To check for doneness, gently pierce the thickest part of the fish with a fork; the fish should flake easily and will be opaque all the way through. Cooking time will vary depending on the size and thickness of the fish fillets.

6. Sprinkle with parsley and serve with lemon wedges for squeezing.

Variation tip: This pecan crust is so versatile. Use it on any mild, firm-flesh white fish, like flounder or crappie, or even chicken breast.

Nutrition information per serving: Calories: 647; Total Fat: 55g; Protein: 27g; Total Carbs: 11g; Net Carbs: 4g; Fiber: 7g; Sodium: 807 mg; Macros: 77% Fat; 17% Protein; 6% Carbs

Southern Oven-Fried
Chicken, page 134

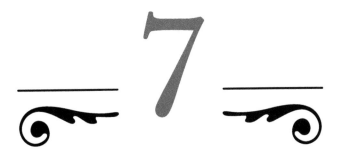

POULTRY

SMOTHERED SOUR CREAM CHICKEN THIGHS

Egg-free, Gluten-free, Nut-free

SERVES 4 / PREP TIME: 15 MINUTES / COOK TIME: 45 MINUTES

Chicken thighs are a versatile, flavorful, and inexpensive protein option for keto. Roasting the chicken and making the sour cream and mushroom sauce in the same pan means minimal cleanup and maximum flavor. Serve this dish over Creamy Mashed "Fauxtatos" (page 68).

4 bone-in, skin-on chicken thighs

Kosher salt

Freshly ground black pepper

Paprika, for seasoning

Garlic powder, for seasoning

8 ounces sliced cremini mushrooms or white button mushrooms

⅓ cup diced onion

¼ cup sherry or white wine

1 cup chicken stock

½ cup heavy (whipping) cream

⅓ cup sour cream

1. Preheat the oven to 375°F.

2. Season both sides of the chicken thighs with salt, pepper, paprika, and garlic powder.

3. Heat a large ovenproof skillet or cast-iron pan over medium-high heat. Place the chicken in the skillet, skin-side down. Cook for 5 to 7 minutes and turn the chicken over.

4. Place the skillet in the oven and roast the chicken for 35 to 40 minutes until the internal temperature reaches 175°F on an instant-read thermometer.

5. Remove the chicken from the skillet and set aside. Remove all but 2 to 3 tablespoons of fat from the pan. Add the mushrooms, onion, and ¼ teaspoon of salt to the skillet. Cook for 5 to 7 minutes until the mushrooms and onion are tender and the mushrooms begin to caramelize.

6. Add the sherry and chicken stock. Simmer for 10 minutes, stirring occasionally and scraping up any bits from the bottom of the pan.

7. Stir in the heavy cream and simmer for 2 to 3 minutes more. Stir in the sour cream and return the chicken thighs to the pan to warm.

Time-saving tip: I love using bone-in chicken thighs because they are inexpensive, flavorful, and stay juicy. But you can cut your cooking time in half by using boneless, skinless thighs, diced. Add 1 tablespoon butter to the pan with the chicken. Cook for 2 to 3 minutes per side until golden and almost completely cooked through. Remove from the pan and prepare the sauce as directed. Add the chicken back to the sauce to finish cooking.

Nutrition information per serving: Calories: 406; Total Fat: 34g; Protein: 20g; Total Carbs: 5g; Net Carbs: 4g; Fiber: 1g; Sodium: 434mg; Macros: 75% Fat; 20% Protein; 5% Carbs

UNSTUFFED BELL PEPPER SKILLET

Egg-free, Gluten-free, Nut-free

SERVES 6 / PREP TIME: 20 MINUTES / COOK TIME: 20 MINUTES

Classic stuffed peppers have always been a family favorite, so I made a quick skillet version that became an instant hit.

2 tablespoons butter or avocado oil

1¼ pounds 85% lean ground turkey

1½ cups diced green bell pepper

½ cup diced onion

2 teaspoons kosher salt, divided

1 teaspoon freshly ground black pepper, divided

1 teaspoon garlic powder, divided

1 (14-ounce) can diced tomatoes

⅓ cup heavy (whipping) cream

2 tablespoons tomato paste

1½ tablespoons Worcestershire sauce

1 (10- or 12-ounce) package frozen cauliflower rice, cooked according to the package directions

1 cup shredded Colby or Cheddar cheese, divided

¼ cup grated Parmesan cheese

1. Preheat the oven to 400°F.

2. In a large ovenproof skillet or cast-iron pan over medium-high heat, melt the butter. Add the ground turkey, green bell pepper, onion, 1 teaspoon of salt, ½ teaspoon of pepper, and ½ teaspoon of garlic powder. Cook for about 8 minutes until the turkey is brown and the vegetables are tender.

3. Stir in the tomatoes, heavy cream, tomato paste, Worcestershire sauce, and remaining 1 teaspoon of salt, ½ teaspoon of pepper, and ½ teaspoon of garlic powder. Cook for 1 to 2 minutes.

4. Stir in the cauliflower rice, ½ cup of Colby cheese, and the Parmesan cheese until fully incorporated. Top with the remaining ½ cup of Colby cheese and place the skillet in the oven.

5. Bake for 7 to 10 minutes, or until bubbly and the cheese is melted.

Nutrition information per serving: Calories: 387; Total Fat: 27g; Protein: 26g; Total Carbs: 10g; Net Carbs: 7g; Fiber: 3g; Sodium: 1067mg; Macros: 63% Fat; 26% Protein; 11% Carbs

WEEKNIGHT TEXAS TURKEY CHILI

Dairy-free, Egg-free, Gluten-free, Nut-free

SERVES 4 / PREP TIME: 15 MINUTES / COOK TIME: 40 MINUTES

When the first little cold spell of the season moves in, it almost requires celebration with a pot of chili. My chili usually simmers for a few hours, but this Texas turkey chili takes just about half an hour and is perfect for a busy weeknight. For me, chili is all about the toppings, so load it up with cheese, avocado, sour cream, and diced onion.

1 tablespoon avocado oil

1¼ pounds 85% lean ground turkey

½ cup chopped onion

½ cup chopped green bell pepper

2 garlic cloves, minced

1 teaspoon kosher salt

1½ tablespoons chili powder

2 teaspoons paprika

1 teaspoon garlic powder

½ teaspoon dried Mexican oregano

½ teaspoon ground cumin

1 (14-ounce) can diced tomatoes

1½ cups water or chicken stock

1 tablespoon tomato paste

Shredded cheese, for garnish

Sour cream, for garnish

Diced avocado, for garnish

Sliced scallion, for garnish

1. In a Dutch oven over medium-high heat, heat the avocado oil. Add the ground turkey, onion, green bell pepper, garlic, and salt. Cook for about 8 minutes until the turkey is brown and cooked through, crumbling it while cooking.

2. Stir in the chili powder, paprika, garlic powder, oregano, and cumin. Cook for 1 minute.

3. Stir in the tomatoes, water, and tomato paste. Simmer, uncovered, for 30 minutes.

4. Serve topped with shredded cheese, sour cream, avocado, and scallion.

Nutrition information per serving: Calories: 540; Total Fat: 40g; Protein: 32g; Total Carbs: 13g; Net Carbs: 7g; Fiber: 6g; Sodium: 813mg; Macros: 67% Fat; 24% Protein; 9% Carbs

HOMESTYLE CHICKEN AND DUMPLINGS

Gluten-free

SERVES 6 / PREP TIME: 20 MINUTES / COOK TIME: 45 MINUTES

Dumplings are traditionally poached in the broth and help thicken the soup. But for this keto version, we bake the dumplings so they hold up in the soup and we have better portion control. My family likes our chicken and dumplings creamy, so I thicken the soup with puréed cauliflower . . . don't worry, it's completely undetectable and will be our secret!

FOR THE DUMPLINGS

¾ cup almond flour

¼ cup coconut flour

½ teaspoon baking powder

¼ teaspoon kosher salt

⅛ teaspoon freshly ground
    black pepper

⅛ teaspoon poultry seasoning

3 eggs, lightly beaten

⅓ cup shredded mozzarella cheese

2½ tablespoons butter, melted

FOR THE CHICKEN STEW

1½ tablespoons butter

1½ cup diced celery

½ cup diced onion

1 teaspoon kosher salt

2 garlic cloves, finely minced

½ teaspoon poultry seasoning

½ tablespoon dried parsley

¼ teaspoon dried thyme

5 cups chicken stock or bone broth

2 cups cauliflower florets

¾ cup heavy (whipping) cream

3 ounces cream cheese

3 cups cooked chicken, turkey,
    dove, or quail

TO MAKE THE DUMPLINGS

1. Preheat the oven to 350°F. Line a baking sheet with parchment paper. Set aside.

2. In a large bowl, stir together the almond and coconut flours, baking powder, salt, pepper, and poultry seasoning. Stir in the eggs, mozzarella cheese, and melted butter until fully incorporated. Let rest for 5 minutes.

3. Using a cookie scoop or spoon, scoop the dough onto the prepared baking sheet (about 18 dumplings). Roll each portion into a ball, if desired.

4. Bake for 10 to 12 minutes, or until slightly golden on the tops. Set aside.

TO MAKE THE CHICKEN STEW

1. In a Dutch oven over medium heat, melt the butter. Add the celery, onion, and salt. Cook for 5 to 7 minutes until the vegetables are tender. Add the garlic, poultry seasoning, parsley, and thyme. Cook for 1 minute more. Add the chicken stock and simmer, uncovered, for 20 minutes.

2. In a medium microwave-safe bowl, combine the cauliflower and ¼ cup water. Cover tightly with plastic wrap and microwave on high power for 5 to 7 minutes, or until tender. Transfer the cauliflower to a blender, and add the heavy cream and cream cheese. Blend on high speed until smooth and creamy. Add the cauliflower mixture to the stock and vegetable mixture. Stir to combine.

3. Add the chicken and cook for about 5 minutes, or until heated through.

4. Place 3 dumplings in a bowl and ladle about 1 cup of chicken stew over the dumplings.

Time-saving tip: Only have frozen cauliflower on hand? No problem! Simply cook the florets for 1 to 2 minutes more, or until tender.

Nutrition information per serving: Calories: 604; Total Fat: 48g; Protein: 30g; Total Carbs: 13g; Net Carbs: 7g; Fiber: 6g; Sodium: 1353mg; Macros: 72% Fat; 20% Protein; 8% Carbs

BACON-WRAPPED CAJUN TURKEY TENDERLOINS WITH ROASTED BRUSSELS SPROUTS

Dairy-free, Egg-free, Gluten-free, Nut-free

SERVES 6 / PREP TIME: 20 MINUTES / CHILL TIME: 4 HOURS / COOK TIME: 45 MINUTES

This turkey dinner is inspired by my favorite Cajun fried turkey. Turkey tenderloins are lean, white meat so I like to wrap them in bacon to add some fat and keep things juicy. Paired with crispy roasted Brussels sprouts, this sheet pan turkey dinner couldn't be easier.

2 turkey tenderloins (about 1¼ pounds total), large tendons removed, if needed

3 teaspoons Cajun seasoning, plus more as needed

2 teaspoons garlic powder, divided

2 teaspoons kosher salt, divided

8 bacon slices

1½ pounds Brussels sprouts, washed, trimmed, and halved

3 tablespoons bacon drippings or avocado oil

½ teaspoon freshly ground black pepper

1. Season the turkey tenderloins on both sides with the Cajun seasoning, 1 teaspoon of garlic powder, and 1 teaspoon of salt. Place them in a zip-top bag and refrigerate for at least 4 hours.

2. Preheat the oven to 400°F. Line a sheet pan with parchment paper. Set aside.

3. Wrap each tenderloin with 4 bacon strips and secure with toothpicks, if needed. Place the wrapped tenderloins on the prepared sheet pan and sprinkle with additional Cajun seasoning, if desired.

4. In a medium bowl, toss together the Brussels sprouts, bacon drippings, the remaining 1 teaspoon each of salt and garlic powder, and the pepper. Place the Brussels sprouts on the sheet pan around the turkey.

5. Bake for about 40 minutes, or until the internal temperature of the turkey reaches 160°F. Broil for 2 to 3 minutes to crisp the bacon, if needed. Let rest for 10 minutes before slicing.

Troubleshooting tip: For best results, use regular or thin-sliced bacon to wrap the tenderloin.

Nutrition information per serving: Calories: 355; Total Fat: 19g; Protein: 35g; Total Carbs: 11g; Net Carbs: 7g; Fiber: 4g; Sodium: 1314mg; Macros: 48% Fat; 39% Protein; 13% Carbs

SOUTHERN OVEN-FRIED CHICKEN

Gluten-free

SERVES 8 / PREP TIME: 20 MINUTES / CHILL TIME: 4 HOURS /
COOK TIME: 50 MINUTES

Fried chicken was Big Granny's specialty and the thing she was best known for at her diner in the 1950s. Back then, a whole order of fried chicken would set you back $1.20. After the diner closed, folks in town would bring chicken over to her house so she could cook it for them. This version of "fried" chicken is baked to eliminate the mess and waste that goes with deep-frying. Coated in almond flour and pork rinds, it's a ketofied family favorite that even Big Granny would love.

½ cup sour cream

¼ cup unsweetened almond milk

2 teaspoons hot sauce

8 bone-in, skin-on chicken thighs

Avocado oil

1 cup almond flour

1 cup crushed pork rinds

⅓ cup grated Parmesan cheese

1 teaspoon paprika

1 teaspoon kosher salt

½ teaspoon garlic powder

½ teaspoon freshly ground
    black pepper

¼ teaspoon cayenne pepper

2 eggs, lightly beaten

1. In a gallon-size, zip-top bag, combine the sour cream, almond milk, and hot sauce. Add the chicken thighs, seal the bag, and shake until the chicken is thoroughly coated. Refrigerate for at least 4 hours, and up to 24 hours.

2. Preheat the oven to 400°F. Line a sheet pan with parchment paper, brush with avocado oil, and set aside.

3. In a shallow dish, stir together the almond flour, pork rinds, Parmesan cheese, paprika, salt, garlic powder, black pepper, and cayenne. Place the eggs in another shallow bowl.

4. Remove the chicken from the bag, place it on paper towels, and pat dry. Dip the chicken into the egg and dredge it in the almond flour mixture, coating all sides. Place the coated chicken, skin-side down, on the prepared sheet pan.

5. Bake for 35 minutes. Flip the chicken and bake for 15 minutes more, or until the chicken reaches 175°F on an instant-read thermometer. Serve warm.

Nutrition information per serving: Calories: 395; Total Fat: 31g; Protein: 26g; Total Carbs: 3g; Net Carbs: 2g; Fiber: 1g; Sodium: 561mg; Macros: 71% Fat; 26% Protein; 3% Carbs

CHICKEN POTPIE BAKE

Gluten-free

SERVES 9 / PREP TIME: 20 MINUTES / COOK TIME: 55 MINUTES

A creamy chicken and vegetable filling topped with crispy drop biscuits, this chicken potpie will be a new family favorite. Turnips create that familiar potato-like texture that makes a potpie so comforting and I even included a few chunks of carrot for nostalgia.

FOR THE FILLING

3 tablespoons butter, plus more for preparing the baking dish

6 boneless, skinless chicken thighs, cut into 1-inch pieces

1 cup diced celery

½ cup diced onion

2 turnips, peeled and cut into ½-inch pieces

1 carrot, diced

1 cup roughly chopped mushrooms

1 teaspoon kosher salt

1 teaspoon dried parsley flakes

½ teaspoon garlic powder

¼ teaspoon dried thyme

¼ teaspoon poultry seasoning

1½ cups chicken stock or bone broth

1 cup frozen cut green beans

¾ cup heavy (whipping) cream

4 ounces cream cheese, at room temperature

FOR THE BISCUIT TOPPING

1½ cups almond flour

2½ tablespoons coconut flour

1 tablespoon baking powder

1½ teaspoons monk fruit/erythritol blend sweetener

½ teaspoon kosher salt

2 eggs, lightly beaten

2 tablespoons sour cream

5 tablespoons butter, melted

TO MAKE THE FILLING

1. Preheat the oven to 350°F. Coat a 9-by-9-inch baking dish with butter. Set aside.

2. In a sauté pan or skillet over medium-high heat, melt the butter. Add the chicken, celery, and onion. Cook for 5 to 7 minutes, stirring constantly, until the chicken is golden brown and the vegetables are tender.

3. Lower the heat to medium. Stir in the turnips, carrot, mushrooms, salt, parsley, garlic powder, thyme, and poultry seasoning. Cook for 3 to 5 minutes more. Add the chicken stock and simmer the mixture uncovered for about 10 minutes until the vegetables are tender.

4. Stir in the green beans and heavy cream. Cook for 3 to 5 minutes until the sauce is thickened. Remove from the heat and stir in the cream cheese until melted. Pour the mixture into the prepared baking dish. Set aside.

TO MAKE THE BISCUIT TOPPING

1. In a medium bowl, stir together the almond and coconut flours, baking powder, sweetener, and salt.

2. Stir in the eggs and sour cream to combine. Pour in the melted butter and stir until fully incorporated. Drop the dough in scant ¼ cup dollops, onto the chicken filling. Flatten slightly if mounded.

3. Bake for 25 to 30 minutes, or until golden brown and bubbly.

Nutrition information per serving: Calories: 445; Total Fat: 33g; Protein: 26g; Total Carbs: 11g; Net Carbs: 6g; Fiber: 5g; Sodium: 388mg; Macros: 67% Fat; 23% Protein; 10% Carbs

POTLUCK CHICKEN SPAGHETTI SQUASH CASSEROLE

Egg-free, Gluten-free, Nut-free

SERVES 8 / PREP TIME: 30 MINUTES / COOK TIME: 50 MINUTES

When my mom entertains a crowd, she whips up a huge batch of chicken spaghetti. Everyone loves it and it's everything you want in a comfort food. This spaghetti squash version has all the amazing flavors of the classic dish minus the carb coma. Great for entertaining and for meal prep, and it's even better the next day.

Olive oil

1 spaghetti squash (about 3 pounds)

Kosher salt

5 tablespoons butter

1 cup diced celery

½ cup diced onion

1 cup diced green bell pepper

½ cup diced poblano pepper

4 garlic cloves, minced

1 (10-ounce) can diced tomatoes and green chilies (like Ro-Tel), drained

⅓ cup chicken stock

1 cup heavy (whipping) cream

5 ounces cream cheese, at room temperature

1 teaspoon ground cumin

½ teaspoon garlic powder

¼ teaspoon freshly ground black pepper

1½ cups shredded Colby cheese

4 cups shredded cooked chicken

1. Preheat the oven to 400°F. Line a sheet pan with parchment paper. Coat a 9-by-13-inch baking pan with olive oil. Set aside.

2. Pierce the squash several times with a fork. Microwave the whole squash for 5 to 7 minutes to soften it slightly. Be careful when removing the squash, as the skin will be hot. Trim off both ends of the squash and cut the squash lengthwise down the middle. Scrape out and discard the seeds. Drizzle the cut sides of the squash with olive oil and season lightly with salt. Place the squash, cut-side down, on the prepared sheet pan.

3. Roast for 30 minutes.

4. While the squash roasts, in a large sauté pan or skillet over medium-high heat, melt the butter. Add the celery, onion, green bell pepper, and poblano. Cook for about 7 minutes, or until softened. Throw in garlic and cook for 1 to 2 minutes more.

5. Stir in the tomatoes and green chilies and chicken stock. Cook for about 4 minutes until reduced by half. You should have about 3 tablespoons of liquid left.

6. Add the heavy cream to the veggies and simmer for 3 to 4 minutes until reduced and thickened. Remove from the heat and transfer the veggie mixture to a large bowl. Stir in the cream cheese, cumin, garlic powder, pepper, and season with salt. Stir until combined and the cream cheese is melted.

7. Remove the squash from the oven and carefully flip it over. It should be tender on top but not completely done all the way through. Using a fork, scrape across the spaghetti squash to create strands. If there is excess moisture in the cooked squash, place the squash on paper towels to remove it.

8. Lower the oven temperature to 350°F.

9. Gently mix the squash into the veggie mixture. Gently stir in ½ cup of Colby cheese and the chicken. Transfer the mixture to the prepared baking pan. Top with the remaining 1 cup of Colby cheese.

10. Bake for 20 minutes, or until warmed through and the cheese is melted and bubbly. Let sit for 10 minutes before digging in!

Nutrition information per serving: Calories: 530; Total Fat: 38g; Protein: 30g; Total Carbs: 17g; Net Carbs: 14g; Fiber: 3g; Sodium: 365mg; Macros: 65% Fat; 23% Protein; 12% Carbs

CHICKEN AND RICE CASSEROLE

Egg-free, Gluten-free, Nut-free

SERVES 6 / PREP TIME: 15 MINUTES / COOK TIME: 35 MINUTES

Chicken and rice casserole is one of my girls' favorites—cheesy, creamy, and loaded with chicken. I make my own quick version of creamy soup and use cauliflower rice for this recipe. But make no mistake, it's as delicious as the original.

2 tablespoons butter, plus more for preparing the baking dish

2 (12-ounce) packages frozen cauliflower rice, cooked according to the package instructions, cooled

¾ cup chopped celery

¾ cup chopped white onion

½ cup chopped white mushrooms

1 cup heavy (whipping) cream

2 cups shredded Colby cheese, divided

¾ cup full-fat sour cream

2 ½ cups shredded cooked chicken

1 ½ teaspoons kosher salt, plus more as needed

1 teaspoon granulated garlic

½ teaspoon freshly ground black pepper, plus more as needed

1. Preheat the oven to 325°F. Coat a 9-by-9-inch baking dish with butter. Set aside.

2. Press the cauliflower rice between paper towels to remove excess moisture. Set aside. You want the rice to be fairly dry so your dish isn't watery.

3. In a sauté pan or skillet over medium-high heat, melt the butter. Add the celery, onion, and mushrooms. Cook for about 7 minutes, or until tender.

4. Reduce the heat to medium and add the heavy cream to the skillet. Cook, stirring constantly, for 4 to 5 minutes to reduce by half, or until thick and creamy. Set aside.

5. In a large bowl, stir together the cauliflower rice, 1½ cups of Colby cheese, the sour cream, vegetable-cream mixture, chicken, salt, granulated garlic, and pepper. Taste and add more salt and pepper, as needed. Spread the mixture evenly in the prepared baking dish and top with the remaining ½ cup of Colby cheese.

6. Bake for 20 to 25 minutes, or until bubbly.

Time-saving tip: When I have a little free time to meal prep, I roast 2 or 3 whole chickens, debone them, and pack the cooked chicken for use in dishes like this one. One chicken yields about 4 cups shredded chicken. Place 2 cups of shredded chicken in a zip-top bag, remove the air, seal, label, and freeze for about 3 months, or refrigerate for 3 to 4 days.

Nutrition information per serving: Calories: 511; Total Fat: 39g; Protein: 29g; Total Carbs: 11g; Net Carbs: 6g; Fiber: 5g; Sodium: 960mg; Macros: 69% Fat; 23% Protein; 8% Carbs

CALABACITAS CON POLLO

Dairy-free, Egg-free, Gluten-free, Nut-free

SERVES 6 / PREP TIME: 15 MINUTES / COOK TIME: 40 MINUTES

When cold weather hits, this squash and chicken dish will warm you from the inside out. The chicken thighs stewed with squash in a spiced-up tomato sauce is a one-pot treat.

1½ pounds boneless, skinless chicken thighs

Kosher salt

Freshly ground black pepper

Garlic powder, for seasoning

2 tablespoons avocado oil, olive oil, or ghee

1 green bell pepper, seeded and diced

½ medium onion, diced

3 garlic cloves, finely minced

2½ teaspoons chili powder

1 teaspoon ground cumin

1 (10-ounce) can diced tomatoes and green chilies (like Ro-Tel)

1 (8-ounce) can tomato sauce

1 cup chicken stock or bone broth

4 Mexican squash or *calabacitas*, halved lengthwise and sliced

1 large yellow squash, halved lengthwise and sliced

Sliced avocado, for garnish

1. Season the chicken with salt, pepper, and garlic powder.

2. In a large sauté pan or skillet, over medium-high heat, heat the avocado oil. Add the chicken and cook for 2 to 3 minutes per side until golden in color. Remove the chicken and set aside to cool. Note that the chicken does not have to be cooked through. When cooled, dice into bite-size pieces and set aside.

3. Return the skillet to the heat and add the green bell pepper and onion. Sauté for 3 to 5 minutes, or until the onion is translucent. Add the garlic, chili powder, 1½ teaspoons salt, and cumin. Sauté for 1 minute, stirring constantly.

4. Reduce the heat to medium and add the tomatoes and green chilies, tomato sauce, chicken stock, Mexican squash, yellow squash, and chicken. Stir to combine. Simmer, uncovered, for 20 to 25 minutes, or until the sauce is thickened and the squash is tender. Serve topped with avocado.

Troubleshooting tip: Calabacitas hold up well to cooking and don't fall apart as easily as other squash. If you can't find Mexican squash or calabacitas, use zucchini.

Nutrition information per serving: Calories: 299; Total Fat: 15g; Protein: 26g; Total Carbs: 15g; Net Carbs: 9g; Fiber: 6g; Sodium: 459mg; Macros: 45% Fat; 35% Protein; 20% Carbs

Cast-Iron Blackened Rib Eye with
Parmesan Roasted Radishes, page 158

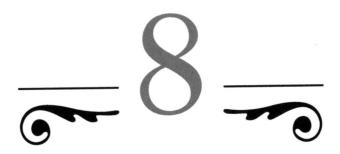

BEEF AND PORK

RANCH FAVORITE TEXAS-STYLE PULLED PORK

Dairy-free, Egg-free, Gluten-free, Nut-free

SERVES 8 / PREP TIME: 15 MINUTES / COOK TIME: 8 HOURS

Pulled pork is a favorite with our ranch guests and a slow cooker makes easy work of this juicy and flavorful pork butt. We love making pulled pork taco bowls topped with my Crisp and Creamy Southern Coleslaw (page 63), chopped fresh cilantro, and a little diced onion.

1 tablespoon paprika

1 tablespoon monk fruit/erythritol blend sweetener

2½ teaspoons kosher salt, divided

1 teaspoon freshly ground black pepper

2 teaspoons garlic powder

1 teaspoon chili powder

1 teaspoon onion powder

½ teaspoon cayenne pepper

½ teaspoon dry mustard

1 (5-pound) bone-in pork butt

2 tablespoons yellow mustard

½ cup diced onion

½ cup sugar-free barbecue sauce

1¼ tablespoons apple cider vinegar

1 tablespoon gluten-free Worcestershire sauce

Diced purple onion, for garnish

Chopped fresh cilantro, for garnish

1. In a small bowl, stir together the paprika, sweetener, 2 teaspoons of salt, the black pepper, garlic powder, chili powder, onion powder, cayenne, and dry mustard.

2. Pat the pork butt dry with paper towels and trim excess fat, if needed. There should be about ⅛ inch of fat on the pork butt. Rub the entire outside of the pork butt with yellow mustard and generously season the pork butt with the spice mix. Rub the seasoning into the roast. Reserve any remaining seasoning.

3. Add the onion to the slow cooker and place the pork butt on top of the onion. Cover the slow cooker and cook on low heat for 8 hours.

4. Remove the pork butt from the cooker. Remove the bone and shred the pork butt with two forks and set aside.

5. Strain the juices from the slow cooker into a small saucepan and bring to a boil over high heat. Cook, uncovered, for about 10 minutes until reduced. Stir in the barbecue sauce, vinegar, Worcestershire sauce, and remaining ½ teaspoon of salt. Pour the sauce over the shredded pork and season with any remaining rub. Serve topped with purple onion and cilantro.

Time-saving tip: If you cook a larger pork roast, you will almost be guaranteed leftovers. Pulled pork freezes beautifully and is great to have in the freezer to help with weekly meal prep. Pack the cooled pulled pork with juice into zip-top bags, remove the air, seal, and label for storage. Freeze for up to 3 months.

Nutrition information per serving: Calories: 504; Total Fat: 40g; Protein: 33g; Total Carbs: 3g; Net Carbs: 2g; Fiber: 1g; Sodium: 491mg; Erythritol Carbs: 1g; Macros: 71% Fat; 26% Protein; 3% Carbs

SAUCY SWEDISH MEATBALLS

Gluten-free

SERVES 8 / PREP TIME: 25 MINUTES / COOK TIME: 45 MINUTES

Swedish meatballs are a favorite comfort food dish and one of our Granny's specialties. She would always serve these meatballs over mashed potatoes, but we love to spoon them, and the amazing gravy, over mashed turnips (see Creamy Mashed "Fauxtatos," page 68) or riced cauliflower to keep it keto-friendly.

FOR THE MEATBALLS

2 tablespoons olive oil, divided

⅓ cup minced purple onion

3 garlic cloves, minced

1 pound 80% lean ground beef

1 pound ground pork

1 tablespoon kosher salt

1 tablespoon coconut flour

2 teaspoons freshly ground black pepper

2 teaspoons garlic powder

2 eggs, beaten

1 tablespoon tomato paste

2 teaspoons gluten-free Worcestershire sauce

1½ teaspoons mayonnaise

FOR THE SAUCE

1 cup sliced mushrooms

¼ cup diced onion

½ teaspoon kosher salt, plus more as needed

1 cup chicken stock

¼ cup sherry

¼ teaspoon paprika

⅛ teaspoon dried thyme

¾ cup heavy (whipping) cream

2 ounces cream cheese, at room temperature

⅓ cup sour cream

Freshly ground black pepper

TO MAKE THE MEATBALLS

1. In a small sauté pan or skillet over medium heat, combine 1 tablespoon of olive oil and the onion. Sauté for about 5 minutes until the onion is translucent. Add the garlic and sauté for 1 minute more. Remove from the heat and set aside.

2. In a large bowl, combine the ground beef, ground pork, onion/garlic mixture, salt, coconut flour, pepper, garlic powder, eggs, tomato paste, Worcestershire sauce, and mayonnaise. Gently combine, without over-working the meat. Form the meat mixture into golf ball–size balls.

3. Preheat a large skillet over medium-high heat. Add the remaining 1 tablespoon of olive oil. Place the meatballs in the skillet and cook for 2 to 3 minutes per side until brown. Note that the meatballs do not have to be cooked through and will finish cooking in the sauce. Repeat until all the meatballs are browned and set them aside.

TO MAKE THE SAUCE

1. Return the skillet to medium-high heat. Add the mushrooms, onion, and salt. Sauté for about 5 minutes until the onion is translucent and the mushrooms are golden brown in color.

2. Stir in the chicken stock, sherry, paprika, and thyme, stirring to scrape up any bits stuck to the bottom of the pan. Reduce the heat to medium and simmer for 5 to 7 minutes.

3. Add the heavy cream and simmer for 3 to 5 minutes more until the sauce starts to thicken.

4. Turn the heat to low and whisk in the cream cheese and sour cream until incorporated.

5. Add the meatballs to the sauce and simmer for 5 to 7 minutes, uncovered, until the meatballs are done and the sauce is thickened. Taste the sauce and add more salt and pepper, as needed.

Nutrition information per serving: Calories: 417; Total Fat: 33g; Protein: 25g; Total Carbs: 5g; Net Carbs: 3g; Fiber: 2g; Sodium: 1031mg; Macros: 71% Fat; 24% Protein; 5% Carbs

SPICED-UP SUNDAY POT ROAST AND SAUTÉED SQUASH

Egg-free, Gluten-free, Nut-free

SERVES 8 / PREP TIME: 20 MINUTES / COOK TIME: 4 HOURS

On Sundays I like to slow down a bit and take time to enjoy the day, which sometimes means putting something on for dinner and just letting it go. There is nothing better for that than pot roast: Fall-apart tender beef, served with tender vegetables and gravy. This pot roast is not only delicious, it's a Sunday tradition. I use a cast-iron Dutch oven that can go from stovetop to oven, but you can use a roasting pan or any casserole dish after browning your roast in a heavy skillet.

FOR THE ROAST

2 teaspoons chili powder

1½ teaspoons kosher salt

1 teaspoon ground cumin

1 teaspoon garlic powder

½ teaspoon freshly ground
 black pepper

1 (3½-pound) boneless chuck roast

2 tablespoons avocado oil

1 onion, diced

1 green bell pepper, diced

3 garlic cloves, smashed

1 canned chipotle pepper in adobo,
 seeded and finely diced

5 tablespoons adobo sauce,
 from the can

½ cups beef stock or bone broth

FOR THE SQUASH

3 tablespoons butter

⅓ cup diced purple onion

2 garlic cloves, finely chopped

4 Mexican calabacitas or
 zucchini, diced

1 teaspoon kosher salt

½ teaspoon ground cumin

¼ teaspoon paprika

Crumbled *queso fresco* cheese,
 for garnish

TO MAKE THE ROAST

1. Preheat the oven to 325°F.

2. In a small bowl, stir together the chili powder, salt, cumin, garlic powder, and pepper. Rub the roast all over with the spices.

3. In a large cast-iron Dutch oven or skillet over medium-high heat, heat the avocado oil. Add the roast and cook for about 3 minutes per side until browned sides. If using a skillet, transfer your roast to a baking dish or roaster and proceed.

4. Add the onion, green bell pepper, garlic, chipotle pepper, adobo sauce, and beef stock. Tightly cover the pan.

5. Bake for 3½ to 4 hours, or until tender. Remove the roast from the pan.

6. Carefully transfer the pan juices and vegetables into a saucepan. Skim off the fat, if desired, and simmer over medium-low heat for 10 to 12 minutes until reduced. Carefully pour the reduced juices into a blender and blend until smooth.

TO MAKE THE SQUASH

In a large sauté pan or skillet over medium-high heat, melt the butter. Add the onion and sauté for about 5 minutes, or until translucent. Add the garlic and cook for 1 minute more. Add the squash, salt, cumin, and paprika. Reduce the heat to medium and sauté for 5 to 7 minutes, or until tender. Serve the roast over the squash and top with gravy and queso fresco.

Nutrition information per serving: Calories: 410; Total Fat: 22g; Protein: 43g; Total Carbs: 10g; Net Carbs: 7g; Fiber: 3g; Sodium: 1133mg; Macros: 48% Fat; 42% Protein; 10% Carbs

STUFFED CORN BREAD CASSEROLE

Gluten-free

SERVES 9 / PREP TIME: 20 MINUTES / COOK TIME: 1 HOUR

When cold weather arrives, this hearty casserole is one of the first to be requested by my girls. This dish features a savory and spicy beef chili–style filling, topped with gooey Cheddar cheese, and a keto corn bread. It's a sure-fire winner!

FOR THE CASSEROLE

2 tablespoons butter, plus more for preparing the baking dish

1 green bell pepper, diced

½ onion, diced

2 pounds ground beef

1½ tablespoons chili powder

1 tablespoon garlic powder

1 tablespoon kosher salt

½ teaspoon paprika

1 (14.5-ounce) can diced tomatoes

2½ tablespoons tomato paste

1½ cups grated Cheddar cheese

FOR THE CORN BREAD TOPPING

1 cup almond flour

2½ tablespoons coconut flour

2½ teaspoons baking powder

1 teaspoon monk fruit/erythritol blend sweetener

½ teaspoon kosher salt

¼ teaspoon baking soda

¼ teaspoon garlic powder

¼ teaspoon onion powder

5 eggs

5 tablespoons butter, melted

2 tablespoons sour cream, plus more for serving

2 scallions, sliced

TO MAKE THE CASSEROLE

1. Preheat the oven to 350°F. Coat a 9-by-9-inch baking dish with butter. Set aside.

2. In a large sauté pan or skillet over medium-high heat, melt the butter. Add the green bell pepper and onion. Sauté for 3 to 4 minutes. Add the ground beef and cook for about 5 minutes until browned.

3. Stir in the chili powder, garlic powder, salt, paprika, tomatoes, and tomato paste. Bring to simmer and cook for 5 minutes. Pour the filling into the prepared pan.

4. Top with the Cheddar cheese. Set aside.

TO MAKE THE CORN BREAD TOPPING

1. In a medium bowl, stir together the almond and coconut flours, baking powder, sweetener, salt, baking soda, garlic powder, and onion powder.

2. Add the eggs, melted butter, and sour cream. Whisk until thoroughly incorporated. Stir in the scallions. Spoon the batter over the meat filling and spread it evenly to the edges.

3. Bake for 30 to 35 minutes until golden brown. Serve warm topped with sour cream.

Variation tip: Ground venison is a great alternative to ground beef in this hearty dish, and the perfect way to use that surplus of venison you may have in your freezer.

Nutrition information per serving: Calories: 434; Total Fat: 30g; Protein: 30g; Total Carbs: 11g; Net Carbs: 7g; Fiber: 4g; Sodium: 1127mg; Erythritol Carbs: 0g; Macros: 62% Fat; 28% Protein; 10% Carbs

OVEN-BAKED COUNTRY-STYLE PORK RIBS

Dairy-free, Egg-free, Gluten-free, Nut-free

SERVES 8 / PREP TIME: 20 MINUTES / CHILL TIME: 3 HOURS /
COOK TIME: 2 HOURS, 45 MINUTES

I have fond memories of my mom baking a pan of these ribs—when you saw them go into the oven you knew you were in for a treat! Flavorful and inexpensive country-style ribs are a fantastic keto option if you're a pork lover. These ribs are baked low and slow in the oven until fork-tender. We like them served "dry," or with no sauce, but you can also dress them up with your favorite sugar-free barbecue sauce.

1½ tablespoons monk fruit/erythritol blend sweetener

1 tablespoon paprika

2 teaspoons kosher salt

2 teaspoons garlic powder

1 teaspoon freshly ground black pepper

1 teaspoon chili powder

1 teaspoon onion powder

½ teaspoon cayenne pepper

½ teaspoon dry mustard

1 small onion, sliced

5 pounds country-style, bone-in ribs

Sugar-free barbecue sauce, for serving

1. In a small bowl, stir together the sweetener, paprika, salt, garlic powder, black pepper, chili powder, onion powder, cayenne, and dry mustard. Sprinkle the rub over the ribs, coating both sides well. Place the ribs in a zip-top bag and refrigerate for at least 3 hours.

2. Preheat the oven to 275°F. Cover a large sheet pan with aluminum foil and line it with parchment paper.

3. Place the ribs on the prepared sheet pan in a single layer. Place the onion over the ribs. Tightly cover everything with foil.

4. Bake for 2 hours.

5. Remove the ribs from the oven and remove the foil. Increase the oven temperature to 350°F. Return the ribs to the oven for 30 to 45 minutes more, or until the ribs are pull-apart tender, basting occasionally with the pan juices.

6. Let sit for about 5 minutes before serving, with your favorite sugar-free barbecue sauce, if desired.

Variation tip: When the weather is nice, take your ribs outside to the grill or smoker. These ribs are best cooked low and slow, so season them and cook them at 250°F to 275°F for 2½ to 3 hours, or until tender and the internal temperature is about 160°F on an instant-read thermometer.

Nutrition information per serving: Calories: 529; Total Fat: 33g; Protein: 55g; Total Carbs: 3g; Net Carbs: 2g; Fiber: 1g; Sodium: 761mg; Erythritol Carbs: 2g; Macros: 56% Fat; 42% Protein; 2% Carbs

SOUTHERN-STYLE SHEPHERD'S PIE

Egg-free, Gluten-free, Nut-free

SERVES 8 / PREP TIME: 20 MINUTES / COOK TIME: 1 HOUR

As a kid, I was always excited to see leftover mashed potatoes after dinner because I knew they would become Mom's shepherd's pie the next day—a casserole that has a meat and gravy filling topped with mashed potatoes. I've seen many variations of this classic dish over the years, but this Southern-inspired keto version gets rave reviews every time it graces the dinner table.

FOR THE TOPPING

1 pound small turnips, peeled and diced

Kosher salt

4 tablespoons butter

2 ounces cream cheese

2 to 3 tablespoons heavy (whipping) cream

Freshly ground black pepper

FOR THE FILLING

1½ pounds ground beef

½ cup diced onion

1½ teaspoons kosher salt

2 teaspoons garlic powder, divided

1 teaspoon freshly ground black pepper, divided

4 cups chopped frozen greens (collard, turnip, or chard)

½ cup beef broth or beef stock

2 tablespoons tomato paste

1 tablespoon gluten-free Worcestershire sauce

¼ teaspoon dried thyme

3 ounces cream cheese

¾ cup shredded Parmesan cheese, divided

TO MAKE THE TOPPING

1. In a medium saucepan, combine the turnips, 1 teaspoon of salt, and enough water to cover. Place the pan over medium-high heat and bring to a boil. Cook the turnips for 12 to 15 minutes until tender. Drain. Return the turnips to the pan and let them sit on the warm burner (turned off) for 2 to 3 minutes to help eliminate excess water.

2. Add the butter, cream cheese, and heavy cream to the turnips. Using a potato masher, mash until smooth. Alternatively, use an immersion blender to blend until smooth. Taste and add more salt or pepper, as needed. Set aside.

TO MAKE THE FILLING

1. Preheat the oven to 375°F.

2. In a cast-iron or ovenproof skillet over medium-high heat, combine the ground beef, onion, salt, 1 teaspoon of garlic powder, and ½ teaspoon of pepper. Cook for 5 to 7 minutes until the beef is brown and the onion is translucent.

3. Add the greens, beef broth or stock, tomato paste, Worcestershire sauce, thyme, and the remaining 1 teaspoon of garlic powder and ½ teaspoon of pepper. Cook for about 5 minutes until the greens are tender.

4. Stir in the cream cheese until melted and the sauce is thickened.

5. Gently stir in ½ cup of Parmesan cheese and remove the skillet from the heat.

6. Spoon the mashed turnips over the meat filling and spread it evenly. Top with the remaining ¼ cup of Parmesan cheese.

7. Bake for 20 to 25 minutes, or until golden brown. Let sit for 5 to 10 minutes before serving.

Troubleshooting tip: If you don't have an ovenproof skillet or cast-iron pan, transfer the cooked filling to a greased casserole dish and top with the mashed turnips as directed.

Nutrition information per serving: Calories: 386; Total Fat: 30g; Protein: 22g; Total Carbs: 7g; Net Carbs: 5g; Fiber: 2g; Sodium: 836mg; Macros: 70% Fat; 23% Protein; 7% Carbs

CAST-IRON BLACKENED RIB EYE WITH PARMESAN ROASTED RADISHES

Egg-free, Gluten-free, Nut-free

SERVES 4 / PREP TIME: 20 MINUTES / COOK TIME: 1 HOUR

Sometimes a simple steak dinner is all that will do. A rib eye is an ideal cut of meat for keto due to its ratio of fat to protein, and paired with Parmesan Roasted Radishes, this is one no-fuss meal that will get everyone excited for dinnertime. Blackening the steak adds spicy flavor and is a nice change of pace—just don't forget to turn on your overhead vent.

FOR THE ROASTED RADISHES

3 (6-ounce) bags fresh radishes, trimmed and halved

3 tablespoons avocado oil or bacon drippings

1 teaspoon kosher salt

½ teaspoon garlic powder

¼ teaspoon paprika

¼ teaspoon freshly ground black pepper

½ cup shredded Parmesan cheese, plus more for garnish

Chopped fresh parsley, for garnish

FOR THE STEAKS

2 (1-pound) 1½-inch-thick rib eye steaks, at room temperature

2 to 4 tablespoons blackening seasoning

2 teaspoons garlic powder

1½ teaspoons kosher salt

3 tablespoons butter

TO MAKE THE ROASTED RADISHES

1. Preheat the oven to 400°F. Line a sheet pan with parchment paper.

2. On the prepared sheet pan, toss together the radishes, avocado oil, salt, garlic powder, paprika, and pepper to coat. Spread into an even layer.

3. Roast for 30 to 35 minutes, stirring once halfway through the roasting time.

4. Evenly sprinkle the radishes with the Parmesan cheese. Roast for 5 minutes more. Transfer to a serving dish and top with more Parmesan cheese and garnish with parsley. Set aside. Leave the oven on.

TO MAKE THE STEAKS

1. Liberally season both sides of the steaks with blackening seasoning, garlic powder, and salt. Let rest for 10 minutes.

2. While the steaks rest, preheat a large heavy cast-iron skillet over medium-high heat and turn on your overhead vent.

3. In the hot skillet, melt the butter. As soon as it melts, put the steaks in the skillet. Cook for 2 to 3 minutes on the first side until browned. Flip the steaks and transfer the skillet to the oven. Cook to your desired doneness. For accurate cooking, use an instant-read thermometer inserted into the center of the steak. For rare, cook for 5 to 7 minutes to an internal temperature of 125°F. For medium-rare, cook for 8 to 9 minutes to an internal temperature of 130°F to 135°F. For medium to medium-well, cook for 8 to 10 minutes to an internal temperature of 145°F to 150°F.

4. Remove the steaks from the pan, cover loosely with aluminum foil, and let rest for 10 minutes. Serve with the roasted radishes.

Troubleshooting tip: For a tender, juicy, steak with maximum flavor, season your steaks up to 3 hours before cooking, cover them, and let them come to room temperature. Do not sear a cold steak. I find that beef can take a little more salt and seasoning, especially when cooking a thick steak, so season your steaks liberally.

Nutrition information per serving: Calories: 852; Total Fat: 72g; Protein: 46g; Total Carbs: 5g; Net Carbs: 3g; Fiber: 2g; Sodium: 1825mg; Macros: 76% Fat; 22% Protein; 2% Carbs

CHICKEN-FRIED STEAK FINGERS WITH GRAVY

Gluten-free

SERVES 6 / PREP TIME: 15 MINUTES / COOK TIME: 20 MINUTES

Growing up, I lived for nights when my mom would pan-fry pork chops or chicken-fried steak and serve them with pan gravy. There was NOTHING better. We don't often fry foods but I make an exception for chicken-fried. Instead of deep-frying, though, we pan-fry these steak fingers in keto-friendly lard or tallow, and serve them with Creamy Mashed "Fauxtatos" (page 68) or cauliflower rice. I love mine with gravy; my husband prefers ketchup—either way, they're delicious!

FOR THE CHICKEN-FRIED STEAK

1 cup almond flour

1 cup crushed pork rinds

⅓ cup grated Parmesan cheese

1 teaspoon paprika

1 teaspoon kosher salt, plus more for seasoning

½ teaspoon garlic powder

½ teaspoon freshly ground black pepper, plus more for seasoning

2 eggs, lightly beaten

2 tablespoons unsweetened almond milk (not vanilla)

1½ pounds (about 4 steaks) cubed beef steak, cut into 1½-inch strips

Lard or tallow, for frying

FOR THE GRAVY

2 tablespoons pan drippings

2 tablespoons finely diced onion

4 ounces cream cheese

1 cup unsweetened almond milk

1¼ cups heavy (whipping) cream

Kosher salt

Freshly ground black pepper

TO MAKE THE CHICKEN-FRIED STEAK

1. In a shallow dish, stir together the almond flour, pork rinds, Parmesan cheese, paprika, salt, garlic powder, and pepper. In another shallow dish, whisk the eggs and almond milk well.

2. Place the steak strips on a layer of paper towels and pat dry. Lightly season with salt and pepper. One at a time, dip the strips into the egg mixture. Then dredge the strips in the almond flour mixture.

3. In a large sauté pan or skillet over medium heat, melt the lard and heat it to 375°F. This will take 3 to 5 minutes. You need about 1½ inches of fat in the pan.

4. Fry the steak strips for 2 to 3 minutes per side, or until golden brown. Drain on paper towels, reserving 2 tablespoons of pan drippings. Serve with the gravy or sugar-free ketchup.

TO MAKE THE GRAVY

1. In a medium sauté pan or skillet over medium heat, combine the reserved pan drippings and onion. Sauté for 2 to 3 minutes.

2. Add the cream cheese and almond milk and cook, stirring, until smooth and the cream cheese is melted.

3. Stir in the heavy cream and simmer the gravy for 3 to 5 minutes, or until thick. Season with salt and pepper, and serve immediately.

How-to tip: Sometimes it's difficult to tell if your oil is the right temperature for frying. Here is a trick my Granny used that works every time. Dip the end of a wooden spoon into the preheated oil. If it starts steadily bubbling, your oil is ready. If it starts spattering and bubbling like crazy, the oil is too hot and should be cooled a bit before frying.

Nutrition information per serving: Calories: 643; Total Fat: 51g; Protein: 40g; Total Carbs: 6g; Net Carbs: 4g; Fiber: 2g; Sodium: 722mg; Macros: 71% Fat; 25% Protein; 4% Carbs

SMOTHERED PORK CHOPS WITH ONION GRAVY

Egg-free, Gluten-free, Nut-free

SERVES 4 / PREP TIME: 15 MINUTES / COOK TIME: 30 MINUTES

These smothered pork chops and gravy are lip-smacking good, so tasty that the pan is quite literally licked clean in my house. Smothered pork chops are typically coated in flour, seared, and simmered in a pan gravy to finish cooking them. For this simple keto version, I skip the flour, sear the pork chops, and create a creamy, flavorful gravy with the onion and pan juices that will blow your mind. Serve with Creamy Mashed "Fauxtatos" (page 68) or simple cauliflower rice.

1 teaspoon kosher salt

½ teaspoon freshly ground black pepper

½ teaspoon garlic powder

½ teaspoon paprika

4 (8-ounce) center cut, ½-inch-thick, bone-in pork chops, patted dry

3 tablespoons butter or ghee

1 onion, sliced

¾ cup chicken stock, beef stock, or bone broth

2 tablespoons sherry or dry white wine

1 garlic clove, finely minced

1 teaspoon Dijon mustard

¼ teaspoon dried thyme

¾ cup heavy (whipping) cream

Chopped fresh parsley, for garnish

1. In a small bowl, stir together the salt, pepper, garlic powder, and paprika. Season the pork chops on both sides with the spices.

2. In a large cast-iron skillet, over medium-high heat, melt the butter. Add the pork chops and sear for 2 to 3 minutes per side, or until browned. Depending on the size of your skillet, you may have to brown the pork chops in batches so you don't crowd the skillet. Remove the browned pork chops from the skillet and set aside.

3. Turn the heat to medium-low and add the onion to the skillet. Cook for about 5 minutes, or until the onion begins to turn translucent.

4. Stir in the chicken stock, sherry, garlic, mustard, and thyme. Cook for 3 to 5 minutes more, until the onion is soft and the liquid is reduced.

5. Add the heavy cream and return the pork chops to the skillet. Simmer for 10 to 15 minutes, or until the pork chops are cooked through—at least 145°F on an instant-read thermometer and with the juices running clear. Remove from the heat.

6. Carefully transfer the pan juices/cream mixture and the onions from the skillet into a blender. Blend until smooth. Pour the gravy over the pork chops and garnish with parsley.

Nutrition information per serving: Calories: 675; Total Fat: 51g; Protein: 49g; Total Carbs: 5g; Net Carbs: 4g; Fiber: 1g; Sodium: 880mg; Macros: 68% Fat; 29% Protein; 3% Carbs

QUICK AND EASY DIRTY RICE SKILLET

Dairy-free, Egg-free, Gluten-free, Nut-free

SERVES 4 / PREP TIME: 15 MINUTES / COOK TIME: 20 MINUTES

The first time I made this dish, I could not keep my family from eating it right out of the pan! This dish gets its color and flavor from the bits stuck to the bottom of the pan that are released when the pan is deglazed with the stock.

3 tablespoons bacon drippings or avocado oil

1 pound 80% lean ground beef

1½ teaspoons kosher salt, divided

1 teaspoon garlic powder, divided

¼ teaspoon freshly ground black pepper

1 cup diced celery

1 cup diced green bell pepper

½ cup diced onion

2 garlic cloves, finely minced

1 teaspoon paprika

¼ teaspoon dried oregano

¼ teaspoon dried thyme

¼ teaspoon cayenne pepper

1 (12-ounce) package frozen cauliflower rice

¼ cup chicken stock or bone broth

Sliced scallion, for garnish

1. In a cast-iron skillet over medium-high heat, heat the bacon drippings. Add the ground beef, 1 teaspoon of salt, ½ teaspoon of garlic powder, and the black pepper. Cook, breaking the meat apart with a spoon, for 5 to 7 minutes until the meat browns and begins to caramelize.

2. Reduce the heat to medium. Add the celery, green bell pepper, and onion. Cook for about 5 minutes, or until the vegetables are tender and the onion is translucent. Add the garlic, paprika, oregano, thyme, and cayenne. Cook for 1 minute more.

3. Add the frozen cauliflower rice, chicken stock, remaining ½ teaspoon of salt, and remaining ½ teaspoon of garlic powder. Stir to combine, scraping up any browned bits stuck to the bottom of the pan. Continue to cook for about 5 minutes, stirring often, until the cauliflower rice is tender and there is no liquid left in the pan. Serve garnished with scallion.

Variation tip: This quick-and-easy dish would be delicious using pork breakfast sausage or even venison in place of the beef.

Nutrition information per serving: Calories: 388; Total Fat: 28g; Protein: 24g; Total Carbs: 10g; Net Carbs: 5g; Fiber: 5g; Sodium: 1032mg; Macros: 65% Fat; 25% Protein; 10% Carbs

COLD FRONT KIELBASA AND CABBAGE SKILLET

Dairy-free, Egg-free, Gluten-free, Nut-free

SERVES 8 / PREP TIME: 15 MINUTES / COOK TIME: 45 MINUTES

Both my husband and I have Polish roots, so this dish takes us right back to our childhoods. Cabbage and sausage get along like peas and carrots, and it's a combination my family just can't get enough of. Both of our grandmothers had a fondness for sauerkraut, which adds a tangy flavor to this dish and is delicious paired with smoked Polish sausage.

2 tablespoons lard or bacon fat

1½ pounds Polish smoked sausage, cut into ½-inch pieces

½ cup diced onion

3 garlic cloves, finely chopped

1 (28- or 32-ounce) jar sauerkraut

1 small head green cabbage, washed, cored, and chopped

1 tablespoon gluten-free Worcestershire sauce

½ teaspoon garlic powder

½ tablespoon dried parsley

Kosher salt

Freshly ground black pepper

1. In a large, deep cast-iron skillet or Dutch oven over medium heat, melt the lard. Add the sausage and cook for 3 to 5 minutes. Add the onion and cook for 3 to 4 minutes, until the sausage begins to caramelize. Add the garlic and cook for 1 minute more.

2. Add the undrained sauerkraut to the sausage and stir to combine, scraping up any brown bits from the bottom of the pan.

3. Stir in the cabbage, Worcestershire sauce, garlic powder, parsley, ½ teaspoon of salt, and ¼ teaspoon of pepper. Cover the pan and reduce the heat to medium-low. Cook for 25 minutes, or until the cabbage is tender, stirring often to prevent burning.

4. Turn the heat to medium and cook, uncovered, stirring often, for 10 minutes more, or until any liquid is reduced and the cabbage begins to caramelize. Taste and add more salt and pepper, as needed. Serve hot.

Variation tip: I often substitute ground beef, pork, or venison for the sausage in this recipe to create a one-pan version of the traditional Polish stuffed cabbage *golabki*. Substitute 2 pounds ground meat, seasoned with salt, pepper, and garlic powder for the sausage and add 1½ tablespoons tomato paste when the cabbage is added, before simmering. I finish the dish with ¼ cup heavy (whipping) cream, stirred in when it gets uncovered to mimic the creaminess that rice imparts to the classic dish. If you're dairy-free, omit the cream.

Nutrition information per serving: Calories: 338; Total Fat: 26g; Protein: 13g; Total Carbs: 13g; Net Carbs: 8g; Fiber: 5g; Sodium: 1450mg; Macros: 70% Fat; 15% Protein; 15% Carbs

TEXAS TACO HASH

Egg-free, Gluten-free, Nut-free

SERVES 5 / PREP TIME: 15 MINUTES / COOK TIME: 20 MINUTES

Taco night is one of the most anticipated nights of the week around here. This easy, Tex-Mex–inspired hash takes taco night to a new level and proves comfort food doesn't have to be complicated or time-consuming.

2 tablespoons avocado oil

1½ pounds 80% lean ground beef

½ cup diced onion

½ cup diced green bell pepper

1½ tablespoons chili powder

1 teaspoon garlic powder

1 teaspoon paprika

1 teaspoon kosher salt

½ teaspoon onion powder

½ teaspoon ground cumin

1 (14-ounce) can diced tomatoes with green chilies (like Ro-Tel)

2 cups frozen cauliflower rice

3 tablespoons heavy (whipping) cream

3 tablespoons sour cream

1 cup shredded Colby cheese

Shredded lettuce, for topping (optional)

Chopped fresh tomato, for topping (optional)

Diced avocado, for topping (optional)

Sliced scallion, for topping (optional)

Black olives, for topping (optional)

1. Preheat the oven to 400°F.

2. In a cast-iron or ovenproof skillet over medium-high heat, heat the avocado oil. Add the ground beef, onion, and green bell pepper. Cook for 5 to 7 minutes until the beef is browned and the vegetables are tender.

3. Stir in the chili powder, garlic powder, paprika, salt, onion powder, and cumin. Cook for 1 minute.

4. Stir in the tomatoes and cauliflower rice. Cook 3 to 5 minutes, stirring often, until the cauliflower rice is tender.

5. Stir in the heavy cream and sour cream, and remove the skillet from the heat. Top with the Colby cheese.

6. Bake for 5 to 7 minutes, or until bubbly and the cheese is melted. Serve garnished, as desired.

Nutrition information per serving: Calories: 550; Total Fat: 42g; Protein: 33g; Total Carbs: 10g; Net Carbs: 7g; Fiber: 3g; Sodium: 1047mg; Macros: 69% Fat; 24% Protein; 7% Carbs

Bourbon Pecan Pie Bars, page 180

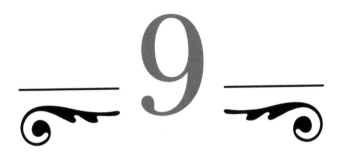

DESSERTS, FAT BOMBS, AND FROZEN DRINKS

LEMONADE SNACK CAKE

Gluten-free, Vegetarian

SERVES 12 / PREP TIME: 15 MINUTES / COOK TIME: 40 MINUTES

This easy snack cake is bright and full of bold flavor. It's delish served with fresh berries and a dollop of whipped cream.

4 tablespoons butter, at room temperature, plus more for preparing the pan

1½ cups almond flour

2 tablespoons coconut flour

2 teaspoons baking powder

½ teaspoon kosher salt

4 ounces cream cheese, at room temperature

½ cup monk fruit/erythritol blend sweetener

4 eggs, at room temperature

1 teaspoon vanilla extract

1½ tablespoons grated lemon zest

1. Preheat the oven to 350°F. Coat a 9-by-5-inch loaf pan with butter. Set aside.

2. In a medium bowl, stir together the almond and coconut flours, baking powder, and salt. Set aside.

3. In another medium bowl and using an electric hand mixer, cream together the butter, cream cheese, and sweetener until fluffy.

4. One at a time, add the eggs, mixing well after each addition. Add the vanilla and lemon zest, and mix to combine.

5. Add the flour mixture and mix until well combined. Pour the batter into the prepared pan.

6. Bake for 35 to 40 minutes, or until a toothpick inserted into the center comes out clean.

7. Let cool in pan for at least 20 minutes before transferring to a wire rack to cool completely before slicing.

Nutrition information per serving: Calories: 152; Total Fat: 13g; Protein: 5g; Total Carbs: 4g; Net Carbs: 2g; Fiber: 2g; Sodium: 176mg; Erythritol Carbs: 8g; Macros: 77% Fat; 13% Protein; 10% Carbs

ITALIAN CREAM CHEESECAKE

Gluten-free, Vegetarian

SERVES 12 / PREP TIME: 15 MINUTES / COOK TIME: 2 HOURS / CHILL TIME: 8 HOURS

What's better than moist, decadent Italian Cream Cake? If you said cheesecake, you're right on! The combination of coconut and pecans is classic, at least in the South, and I think that's why we love Italian Cream Cake so much. The classic version is a three-layer cake studded with pecans and coconut, and frosted with a cream cheese icing. This dreamy dessert has all the flavors of the traditional cake in cheesecake form. As Paige likes to say, "It's like heaven in your mouth!"

FOR THE CRUST

Nonstick cooking spray

1½ cups almond flour

6 tablespoons butter, melted

3 tablespoons monk fruit/erythritol blend sweetener

¼ teaspoon rum extract

Pinch kosher salt

FOR THE CHEESECAKE

3 (8-ounce) packages cream cheese, at room temperature

½ cup monk fruit/erythritol blend sweetener

4 eggs, at room temperature

¾ cup sour cream, at room temperature

½ cup full-fat canned coconut milk

2 teaspoons vanilla extract

1½ teaspoon coconut extract

½ cup toasted pecans, finely chopped

TO MAKE THE CRUST

1. Preheat the oven to 350°F. Lightly coat a 9-inch springform pan with cooking spray and line it with parchment paper. Set aside.

2. In a medium bowl, stir together the almond flour, melted butter, sweetener, rum extract, and salt until crumbly. Firmly press the crust mixture evenly into the bottom and 1 inch up the sides of the prepared pan.

(Continued)

3. Bake for 10 to 12 minutes on the center rack, or until golden brown around the edges. Set the pan aside to cool completely.

TO MAKE THE CHEESECAKE

1. Wrap the outside of a springform pan tightly in two layers of foil to prevent water from leaking in during baking.

2. Lower the oven temperature to 325°F. Place a roaster pan or a pan large enough for the springform pan to fit into on the center oven rack and fill it with about 1 inch of hot water. This will act as a water bath for the cheesecake.

3. In the bowl of a stand mixer fitted with the paddle attachment, or in a large bowl and using an electric hand mixer, beat the cream cheese at medium speed until creamy. Add the sweetener and mix well to combine. One at a time, add the eggs, beating just until incorporated after each addition.

4. Gently stir in the sour cream, coconut milk, vanilla, and coconut extract to combine. Stir in the toasted pecans. Pour the batter onto the prepared crust.

5. Place the wrapped springform pan carefully into the center of the water bath. Bake for 60 to 70 minutes. The outer edges of the cheesecake will be set but the center of the cheesecake will be slightly jiggly and not completely set. Turn off the oven, leaving the door closed, and let the cheesecake sit in the oven for an additional 25 minutes more.

6. Remove the springform pan from the water bath and the foil, and let cool for 15 to 20 minutes on a wire rack. Run a butter knife around the edge of the pan to release the cheesecake from the springform pan and cool completely before covering.

7. Cover the cheesecake and chill for at least 8 hours, or overnight. Carefully remove the sides of the springform pan and transfer the cheesecake to a serving platter.

Time-saving tip: Cheesecakes freeze beautifully, so if you want to serve this cheesecake for a gathering or party, make it ahead. Simply chill it down as stated in the recipe, remove it from the pan, and place it on a cardboard cake circle. Wrap it well with plastic wrap or aluminum foil and freeze for up to 1 month. Thaw in the refrigerator the day before serving.

Troubleshooting tip: To prevent cracks in your cheesecake, make sure all your ingredients are at room temperature. In addition, do not whip or overbeat your batter, beating in the eggs just until incorporated. Over-beating will add too much air to the batter and lead to cracks. A water bath creates an ultra-creamy cheesecake. If you do not have a pan large enough to create a water bath for the cheesecake, place a 9-by-13-inch pan with about an inch of hot water on the oven rack beneath the cheesecake and bake as directed.

Nutrition information per serving: Calories: 416; Total Fat: 40g; Protein: 9g; Total Carbs: 5g; Net Carbs: 4g; Fiber: 1g; Sodium: 241mg; Erythritol Carbs: 11g; Macros: 87% Fat; 9% Protein; 4% Carbs

GRANNY'S BLACKBERRY COBBLER

Gluten-free, Vegetarian

SERVES 9 / PREP TIME: 15 MINUTES / COOK TIME: 30 MINUTES

There is nothing better than a fresh cobbler to showcase gorgeous seasonal fruit. Well, this isn't your traditional "crust and fruit filling" cobbler—this is Texas cobbler, or buckle, and is based on my Granny's famous version that's made with fresh fruit nestled in a rich, buttery cake batter. In the oven, the batter bakes up around all the fruit, creating more of a cake-like dessert with gorgeous, crispy edges.

Nonstick cooking spray

1½ cups almond flour

¼ cup plus 2 tablespoons coconut flour

½ cup plus 1 tablespoon monk fruit/erythritol blend sweetener, divided

1 tablespoon baking powder

½ teaspoon kosher salt

3 eggs, beaten

¾ cup unsweetened almond milk

2 tablespoons sour cream

1 teaspoon vanilla extract

½ cup (1 stick) butter, melted

1 cup fresh blackberries

¼ teaspoon ground cinnamon

Fresh whipped cream, for serving

1. Preheat the oven to 350°F. Coat a 9-by-9-inch square pan with cooking spray. Set aside.

2. In a medium bowl, stir together the almond and coconut flours, ½ cup of sweetener, the baking powder, and salt.

3. Whisk in the eggs, almond milk, sour cream, and vanilla. Continue whisking until the batter is smooth. Stir in the melted butter until fully incorporated. The batter will be thick.

4. Pour the batter into the prepared pan. Evenly sprinkle the blackberries over the batter and push them down slightly. In a small bowl, stir together the remaining 1 tablespoon of sweetener and the cinnamon. Evenly sprinkle the cinnamon mixture over the top of the cobbler.

5. Bake for 25 to 30 minutes, or until the top is golden brown. Let cool for 30 minutes before serving with fresh whipped cream.

How-to tip: To make a quick and easy whipped cream, in a medium bowl and using an electric hand mixer, beat 1 cup heavy (whipping) cream at medium speed; when the cream starts to thicken add 2 teaspoons to 1 tablespoon powdered monk fruit/erythritol blend sweetener and ½ teaspoon vanilla extract. Beat until soft peaks form. Taste and add more sweetener to suit your taste. Don't over-whip or your fluffy whipped cream will turn to butter.

Nutrition information per serving: Calories: 243; Total Fat: 19g; Protein: 6g; Total Carbs: 12g; Net Carbs: 6g; Fiber: 6g; Sodium: 243mg; Erythritol Carbs: 12g; Macros: 70% Fat; 10% Protein; 20% Carbs

FLUFFY PEANUT BUTTER PIE

Egg-free, Gluten-free, Vegetarian

SERVES 8 / PREP TIME: 15 MINUTES / COOK TIME: 12 MINUTES /
CHILL TIME: 3 HOURS

Let's face it, chocolate and peanut butter are one of the tastiest flavor combinations EVER. This delicious dessert pairs an easy, crisp chocolate crust with a light, creamy, no-bake peanut butter filling that results in a pie that's so good it will make you cry. Top with whipped cream and chocolate shavings, and you have one satisfying keto dessert!

1½ cups almond flour

3 tablespoons monk fruit/erythritol blend sweetener

2 tablespoons cocoa powder

4 tablespoons butter, melted

8 ounces cream cheese, at room temperature

½ cup creamy peanut butter

⅓ cup powdered monk fruit/erythritol blend (confectioners' sugar style)

1 cup plus 2 tablespoons heavy (whipping) cream, divided

1 teaspoon vanilla extract

Pinch kosher salt

Fresh whipped cream, for serving (optional)

Sugar-free chocolate shavings, for garnish (optional)

1. Preheat the oven to 350°F.

2. In a medium bowl, stir together the almond flour, sweetener, cocoa powder, and melted butter to combine. Press the mixture firmly into the bottom and up the sides of a 9-inch pie plate.

3. Bake for 10 to 12 minutes. Set aside to cool.

4. In a large bowl and using an electric hand mixer, combine the cream cheese, peanut butter, sweetener, 2 tablespoons of heavy cream, the vanilla, and salt. Beat at medium speed until smooth.

5. In a medium bowl, beat the remaining 1 cup of heavy cream at medium speed until firm peaks form. Gently fold the whipped cream into the cream cheese mixture. Spoon the filling into the prepared crust. Chill for at least 3 hours before serving.

6. Garnish with whipped cream (if using) and chocolate shavings (if using). Refrigerate leftovers in an airtight container for up to 4 days.

Allergen tip: Peanut allergy? Almond butter is a delicious substitute for the peanut butter.

Nutrition information per serving: Calories: 450; Total Fat: 42g; Protein: 10g; Total Carbs: 8g; Net Carbs: 5g; Fiber: 3g; Sodium: 236mg; Erythritol Carbs: 14g; Macros: 84% Fat; 9% Protein; 7% Carbs

BOURBON PECAN PIE BARS

Gluten-free, Vegetarian

SERVES 12 / PREP TIME: 15 MINUTES / COOK TIME: 35 MINUTES

In the South, pecans are a prized possession. I remember picking
up buckets of pecans out of my grandma's backyard. At night, when
I should have been in bed, she would let me help her shell them in the
kitchen while watching her favorite late-night TV show. Nothing quite
showcases pecans like pecan pie and it's pretty much a staple on a Southern
table during any holiday celebration. I always add a little bourbon
to my pecan pie, so these bars are spiked, too!

Nonstick cooking spray

1 cup almond flour

3 tablespoons coconut flour

2 tablespoons monk fruit/erythritol
blend sweetener

¼ teaspoon ground cinnamon

Kosher salt

8 tablespoons (1 stick) butter,
melted, divided

2 eggs, beaten

⅔ cup allulose blend sweetener

¼ cup heavy (whipping) cream

2 tablespoons bourbon

1 teaspoon vanilla extract

1½ cups chopped pecans

1. Preheat the oven to 350°F. Lightly coat an 8-by-8-inch baking pan with
   cooking spray. Set aside.

2. In a medium bowl, stir together the almond and coconut flours, monk
   fruit or erythritol sweetener blend, cinnamon, and a pinch of salt; mix
   well. Stir in 4 tablespoons of melted butter and press the mixture firmly
   into the bottom of the prepared pan.

3. Bake the crust for 8 to 10 minutes until it is golden brown around
   the edges.

4. In another medium bowl, whisk the eggs, allulose blend sweetener, heavy
   cream, remaining 4 tablespoons of melted butter, the bourbon, vanilla,
   and ¼ teaspoon salt until blended well.

5. Sprinkle the pecans evenly over the crust. Pour the egg mixture over the pecans.

6. Bake for 20 to 25 minutes, or until set.

7. Cool completely in the pan before cutting into 12 bars. These bars cut even better after being refrigerated for about an hour and can be stored in the refrigerator until serving.

How-to tip: To easily remove your bars from the pan, lightly spray the pan with coconut oil spray. Line the pan with parchment paper (about 8 inches wide and 12 inches long), so the bottom of the pan is covered, and the parchment slightly overhangs two sides. When the bars are completely cool, carefully run a knife around the edge of the pan and use the parchment to lift the bars out onto a cutting board.

Nutrition information per serving: Calories: 258; Total Fat: 24g; Protein: 4g; Total Carbs: 6g; Net Carbs: 2g; Fiber: 4g; Sodium: 69mg; Erythritol Carbs: 14g; Macros: 84% Fat; 6% Protein; 10% Carbs

BUTTER RUM POUND CAKE

Gluten-free, Vegetarian

SERVES 15 / PREP TIME: 15 MINUTES / COOK TIME: 50 MINUTES TO
1 HOUR, 10 MINUTES

Rum cake is always a favorite around the holidays. This moist pound cake is made with browned butter for extra richness, and then soaked with a rum glaze so tasty it would make your boots taste good! For maximum flavor, make this cake the day before you want to serve it.

FOR THE POUND CAKE

Nonstick cooking spray

7 tablespoons butter

1 cup almond flour

¾ cup coconut flour

⅔ cup monk fruit/erythritol blend sweetener

2 teaspoons baking powder

1 teaspoon baking soda

½ teaspoon kosher salt

8 eggs

¼ cup plus 2 tablespoons sour cream

¼ cup dark rum

1 teaspoon vanilla extract

Fresh whipped cream, for serving

FOR THE GLAZE

4 tablespoons butter

¼ cup allulose blend sweetener

3 tablespoons dark rum

2 tablespoons water

TO MAKE THE POUND CAKE

1. Preheat the oven to 350°F. Coat an 8-inch loaf pan with cooking spray and line it with parchment paper, or spray a 10-cup Bundt pan.

2. In a small skillet over medium-low heat, melt the butter and cook it for about 10 minutes, stirring often, until browned and nutty. The solids in the butter should be the color of caramel. Remove from the heat and set aside to cool.

3. In a medium bowl, stir together the almond and coconut flours, sweetener, baking powder, baking soda, and salt.

4. In the bowl of a stand mixer fitted with the whisk attachment, or in a large bowl and using an electric hand mixer, whip the eggs for about 2 minutes until light and foamy. Add the flour mixture and mix on medium speed until combined, stopping to scrape down the sides.

5. Add the sour cream, rum, vanilla, and cooled browned butter to the batter (reserve the skillet for the glaze) and mix again until well combined.

6. Spoon the batter evenly into the prepared pan and smooth the top.

7. Bake for 45 to 60 minutes (8-inch loaf pan), or 35 to 40 minutes (Bundt pan), or until a toothpick inserted into the center comes out clean. If needed, loosely cover with aluminum foil halfway through the baking time to prevent over-browning.

TO MAKE THE GLAZE

1. While the cake bakes, in the skillet used to brown the butter, combine the butter, sweetener, rum, and water. Place the skillet over medium heat and bring the mixture to a boil. Cook for 2 to 3 minutes.

2. Pour the glaze evenly over the warm cake. Cool the cake in the pan. Turn the cake out onto a cake stand or plate of choice. If you baked this in a loaf pan, use the parchment to lift the loaf out of the pan. Serve with a dollop of whipped cream and enjoy.

3. This cake can be stored and covered at room temperature for up to 4 days.

Troubleshooting tip: I've used both types of sweeteners for this cake and both work well. The monk fruit/erythritol blend sweetener can also be used in the glaze for the cake, in the same amount listed, if you don't have the allulose sweetener available.

Nutrition information per serving: Calories: 179; Total Fat: 15g; Protein: 5g; Total Carbs: 6g; Net Carbs: 3g; Fiber: 3g; Sodium: 260mg; Erythritol Carbs: 12g; Macros: 75% Fat; 11% Protein; 13% Carbs

STRAWBERRY CREAM PIE

Egg-free, Gluten-free

SERVES 8 / PREP TIME: 20 MINUTES / COOK TIME: 36 MINUTES /
CHILL TIME: 5 HOURS

There's a little town in Texas called Poteet, that's famous for strawberries, and during April you can pick up the most amazing strawberries by the flat. My family has a long history in this tiny Texas town and, needless to say, we have a definite love of fresh, juicy strawberries. The addition of vinegar helps intensify the flavor of the berries, so even if you're using fruit that is out of season, the berry flavor really shines through in this creamy strawberry pie.

FOR THE CRUST

Nonstick cooking spray

4½ tablespoons butter

1½ cups almond flour

2 tablespoons monk fruit/erythritol blend sweetener

Pinch kosher salt

FOR THE FILLING

4 tablespoons water, divided

1½ teaspoons gelatin

1½ cups sliced fresh strawberries

3 tablespoons monk fruit/erythritol blend sweetener

1 teaspoon balsamic vinegar

8 ounces cream cheese, at room temperature

¼ cup sour cream

3 tablespoons powdered monk fruit/erythritol blend sweetener

1 teaspoon vanilla extract

1 cup heavy (whipping) cream, whipped, plus more for garnish

Whole fresh strawberries, for garnish

TO MAKE THE CRUST

1. Preheat the oven to 350°F. Lightly coat a 9-inch pie plate with cooking spray. Set aside.

2. In a small sauté pan or skillet over medium-low heat, melt the butter and cook it for about 10 minutes, stirring often, until browned and nutty. The solids in the butter should be the color of caramel. Remove from heat and set aside to cool slightly.

3. In a medium bowl, stir together the almond flour, sweetener, salt, and browned butter to combine. Press the mixture firmly into the bottom and up the sides of the prepared pie plate.

4. Bake for 12 to 14 minutes, or until the edges are golden. Set aside to cool.

TO MAKE THE FILLING

1. Place the 2 tablespoons of water in a small bowl and sprinkle the gelatin on top. Let sit for 5 minutes.

2. In a medium saucepan over medium heat, combine the strawberries, remaining 2 tablespoons of water, 3 tablespoons of the sweetener, and vinegar. Bring to a boil, using a masher to break up the strawberries. Turn the heat to medium-low and simmer the strawberries for 10 to 12 minutes, or until thick. Remove from heat and stir in the gelatin mixture until fully dissolved. Set aside to cool to room temperature.

3. In a medium bowl and using an electric hand mixer, beat the cream cheese, sour cream, powdered sweetener, and vanilla until smooth. Stir in the strawberry mixture until well combined. Gently fold in the whipped cream. Spoon the filling into the prepared crust, cover with plastic wrap, and refrigerate for 3 to 5 hours.

4. Garnish as desired with whipped cream and strawberries.

Nutrition information per serving: Calories: 371; Total Fat: 35g; Protein: 7g; Total Carbs: 7g; Net Carbs: 5g; Fiber: 2g; Sodium: 171mg; Erythritol Carbs: 12g; Macros: 85% Fat; 8% Protein; 7% Carbs

"BUTTERMILK" CUSTARD PIE BARS

Gluten-free

SERVES 12 / PREP TIME: 20 MINUTES / COOK TIME: 45 MINUTES /
CHILL TIME: 3 HOURS

Buttermilk pie is a Southern staple during the holidays and one of my all-time favorites! Traditional buttermilk pie is, of course, made with cultured buttermilk, which gives the pie its tangy flavor. The combination of the heavy cream, vinegar, and sour cream in this recipe takes the place of buttermilk and creates a velvety, creamy custard filling that is sure to put a smile on your face.

FOR THE CRUST

Nonstick cooking spray

1½ cups almond flour

2 tablespoons monk fruit/erythritol blend sweetener

⅛ teaspoon ground nutmeg

Pinch kosher salt

4 tablespoons butter, melted

FOR THE FILLING

1½ cups heavy (whipping) cream

1½ teaspoon white vinegar

6 eggs

⅓ cup allulose blend sweetener

¼ cup coconut flour

¼ cup sour cream

4 tablespoons butter, melted

2 teaspoons vanilla extract

¼ teaspoon ground nutmeg

Pinch kosher salt

TO MAKE THE CRUST

1. Preheat the oven to 350°F. Coat a 9-by-9-inch square pan with cooking spray and line it with parchment paper. Set aside.

2. In a medium bowl, stir together the almond flour, monk fruit/erythritol sweetener blend, nutmeg, salt, and melted butter until incorporated and crumbly. Pour the crust mixture into the prepared pan and evenly press into the bottom.

3. Bake for 8 to 10 minutes until golden brown around the edges. Set aside.

TO MAKE THE FILLING

1. Lower the oven temperature to 325°F.

2. In a small bowl, whisk the heavy cream and vinegar. Let sit for 5 minutes.

3. In a large bowl, whisk the eggs, allulose blend sweetener, coconut flour, sour cream, melted butter, vanilla, nutmeg, salt, and heavy cream mixture. Pour the filling over the crust.

4. Bake for 30 to 35 minutes, or until set. If needed, place a piece of aluminum foil over the top of the bars to prevent over-browning. Don't overbake.

5. Let the bars cool at room temperature. Refrigerate for at least 3 hours before cutting. To serve, lift the bars from the pan using the parchment paper and place on a cutting board. Cut into 12 bars.

Troubleshooting tip: Buttermilk pie is traditionally on the sweeter side of things, so I like using the allulose blend sweetener to sweeten the filling to prevent any heavy crystallization, but it does tend to brown more quickly than when using the monk fruit/erythritol blend sweetener. So, cover the pan lightly with foil, if needed, to prevent over-browning. I have also used the monk fruit/erythritol blend sweetener in this recipe with great results, but the top of the bars will have more crystallization.

Nutrition information per serving: Calories: 282; Total Fat: 26g; Protein: 6g; Total Carbs: 6g; Net Carbs: 3g; Fiber: 3g; Sodium: 114mg; Erythritol Carbs: 7g; Macros: 83% Fat; 9% Protein; 8% Carbs

CHEWY "NOATMEAL" CHOCOLATE CHIP COOKIES

Gluten-free

MAKES 20 COOKIES / PREP TIME: 15 MINUTES / COOK TIME: 18 MINUTES

No keto recipe box is complete without a delicious chocolate chip cookie. The recipe for this treat was years in the making. This cookie is crisp on the outside and chewy in the middle—just like a cookie should be. The addition of gelatin and almond butter creates a delicious chewy texture and the coconut gives the feel of oatmeal without the oats. These cookies come together in just a few minutes and, trust me, the whole family will go crazy for 'em!

½ cup (1 stick) butter

¼ cup creamy almond butter

⅓ cup plus 1 tablespoon monk fruit/ erythritol blend sweetener

1 egg

1 teaspoon vanilla extract

1¼ cups almond flour

1 tablespoon unflavored gelatin

¾ teaspoon baking soda

¼ teaspoon kosher salt

½ cup sugar-free chocolate chips

⅓ cup unsweetened desiccated coconut

1. Preheat the oven to 350°F. Line a baking sheet with parchment paper. Set aside.

2. In a small sauté pan or skillet over medium-low heat, melt the butter and cook it for about 10 minutes, stirring often, until browned and nutty. The solids in the butter should be the color of caramel. Remove from the heat and set aside to cool.

3. In the bowl of a stand mixer fitted with the paddle attachment, or in a large bowl and using an electric hand mixer, cream together the browned butter, almond butter, and sweetener until light and fluffy. Add the egg and vanilla, and mix until combined.

4. Add the almond flour, gelatin, baking soda, and salt. Mix well until thoroughly incorporated.

5. Stir in the chocolate chips and coconut. Scoop the cookies onto the prepared sheet pan, about 1 generous tablespoon each, and flatten slightly.

6. Bake for 7 to 8 minutes, or until golden around the edges.

7. Let cool on the sheet pan for at least 10 minutes before removing. Store in an airtight container.

Variation tip: For a skillet chocolate chip cookie, place the dough in a lightly greased 9-inch cast-iron skillet and bake at 350°F for 25 to 30 minutes, or until golden brown on the edges and slightly gooey in the center. Top with your favorite keto ice cream.

Nutrition information per serving (1 cookie): Calories: 99; Total Fat: 9g; Protein: 2g; Total Carbs: 2g; Net Carbs: 1g; Fiber: 1g; Sodium: 127mg; Erythritol Carbs: 4g; Macros: 84% Fat; 8% Protein; 8% Carbs

SALTED CARAMEL FUDGE FAT BOMBS

Less than 5 Ingredients, Egg-free, Gluten-free, Nut-free, Vegetarian

SERVES 32 / PREP TIME: 15 MINUTES / COOK TIME: 8 MINUTES / CHILL TIME: 1 HOUR

In my family, no holiday is complete without fudge. My mom would typically set aside a whole day for her holiday fudge-making extravaganza and I was always there to sample and lick the spoons. Well, this keto fudge combines my love of salted caramel and dark chocolate into swoon-worthy fat bombs that put traditional fudge to shame . . . sorry, mom!

4 ounces unsweetened chocolate, roughly chopped

8 tablespoons (1 stick) butter

½ cup allulose blend sweetener

½ cup heavy (whipping) cream

Sea salt

1. Line an 8- or 9-inch loaf pan with plastic wrap. Set aside.

2. Place the chocolate in a medium heat-resistant bowl. Set aside.

3. In a saucepan over medium heat, combine the butter and sweetener. Melt the butter and bring the mixture to a boil. Cook for 3 to 5 minutes, or until golden, stirring often.

4. Add the cream and cook for 2 to 3 minutes more. Stir in a pinch of salt. Set aside to cool for 5 to 7 minutes.

5. Pour the warm butter mixture over the chopped chocolate. Let sit for 1 minute. Stir until smooth and the chocolate is completely melted. Immediately pour the fudge into the prepared loaf pan and spread it evenly. Sprinkle the top of the fudge with salt. Refrigerate for 45 minutes to 1 hour, or until firm.

6. Cut the fudge into 32 pieces and keep refrigerated in an airtight container or in the freezer. This fudge can be served at room temperature once it's been completely chilled.

Nutrition information per serving (1 fat bomb): Calories: 62; Total Fat: 6g; Protein: 1g; Total Carbs: 1g; Net Carbs: 0g; Fiber: 1g; Sodium: 31mg; Sweetener Carbs: 3g; Macros: 88% Fat; 6% Protein; 6% Carbs

BUTTER PECAN CHEESECAKE TRUFFLE FAT BOMBS

Less than 5 Ingredients, Egg-free, Gluten-free, Vegetarian

SERVES 24 / PREP TIME: 10 MINUTES / COOK TIME: 5 MINUTES /
CHILL TIME: 20 MINUTES

Growing up, our freezer always had a half-gallon of butter pecan ice cream because it was my mom's favorite flavor. Rich, buttery, and smooth with caramel notes, the flavor seems like it should be complicated to create but it couldn't be easier. The tart cream cheese in these fat bombs is the perfect pairing for the rich butter pecan flavor.

3 tablespoons butter

¼ cup finely chopped pecans

8 ounces cream cheese, at room temperature

3 tablespoons powdered monk fruit/erythritol blend sweetener (confectioners' sugar style)

1 teaspoon vanilla extract

1. In a sauté pan or skillet over medium-low heat, melt the butter. Add the pecans and cook for 3 to 4 minutes, stirring often, until the pecans are toasted and the butter is golden. Set aside the pan to cool.

2. In a medium bowl and using an electric hand mixer, beat the cream cheese, sweetener, and vanilla until smooth. Stir in the pecans and browned butter. Cover and refrigerate the mixture for 15 to 20 minutes, or until firm enough to roll.

3. Drop by the ½ tablespoon onto parchment paper and roll each portion into a ball. Refrigerate in an airtight container for up to 5 days.

Troubleshooting tip: The powdered or confectioners' style monk fruit/erythritol blend sweetener that I use is twice as sweet as sugar, so if using another brand make sure it's also 2:1.

Nutrition information per serving (1 fat bomb): Calories: 62; Total Fat: 6g; Protein: 1g; Total Carbs: 1g; Net Carbs: 1g; Fiber: 0g; Sodium: 38mg; Erythritol Carbs: 2g; Macros: 88% Fat; 6% Protein; 6% Carbs

COWBOY COOKIE DOUGH FAT BOMBS

Egg-free, Gluten-free, Vegetarian

SERVES 12 / PREP TIME: 10 MINUTES / COOK TIME: 5 MINUTES / CHILL TIME: 20 MINUTES

If you're like me, you have fond memories of eating gobs of cookie dough as a child. These cookie dough morsels are full of flavor and are the perfect bite-size treat when you just need a little something sweet.

3 tablespoons butter

⅓ cup almond flour

1 teaspoon coconut flour

1 tablespoon plus 1 teaspoon monk fruit/erythritol blend sweetener

1 ounce cream cheese, at room temperature

½ teaspoon vanilla extract

⅛ teaspoon ground cinnamon

Pinch kosher salt

3 tablespoons sugar-free semisweet chocolate chips, roughly chopped

2 tablespoons finely chopped pecans

1 tablespoon desiccated unsweetened coconut

1. In a small skillet over medium-low heat, melt the butter and cook it for 4 to 6 minutes, stirring often, until the butter starts to foam. The solids in the butter should be the color of caramel and the aroma should be nutty. Cook for 1 minute more and remove the pan from the heat. Set aside to cool.

2. In a medium bowl, stir together the cooled browned butter, almond and coconut flours, sweetener, cream cheese, vanilla, cinnamon, and salt to combine.

3. Stir in the chocolate chips, pecans, and coconut. Refrigerate the dough for 15 to 20 minutes, or until firm.

4. Drop the dough by the ½ tablespoon onto a piece of parchment paper and roll each portion into a ball. Refrigerate in an airtight container for up to 5 days.

Nutrition information per serving: Calories: 53; Total Fat: 5g; Protein: 1g; Total Carbs: 1g; Net Carbs: 0g; Fiber: 1g; Sodium: 40mg; Erythritol Carbs: 1g; Macros: 86% Fat; 7% Protein; 7% Carbs

TRIPLE BERRY COCONUT SMOOTHIE

Less than 30 Minutes, Dairy-free, Egg-free, Gluten-free, Vegan

SERVES 1 / PREP TIME: 10 MINUTES

Smoothies are a quick, easy, and tasty option for breakfast, lunch, or even dessert. The combination of berries and coconut in this rich, creamy smoothie is so delicious it's hard to believe it's dairy-free. For best results, be sure to use full-fat coconut milk and not the coconut beverage found in the refrigerated section.

⅓ cup unsweetened almond milk

⅓ cup full-fat canned coconut milk

⅓ cup frozen whole mixed berries

1 to 2 teaspoons powdered monk fruit/erythritol blend sweetener

1½ teaspoons coconut oil (optional)

¼ teaspoon vanilla extract

Pinch kosher salt

4 or 5 ice cubes

In a blender (high speed is best), combine the almond and coconut milks, frozen berries, sweetener, coconut oil (if using), vanilla, and salt. Blend on high speed until smooth and creamy. Add the ice and blend again until your desired consistency is reached. Pour into a glass and enjoy!

Troubleshooting tip: The amount of sweetener used may vary depending on the sweetness of your berries and your personal taste. Start with the smallest amount of sweetener and add more until you get your sweetness level.

Nutrition information per serving: Calories: 206; Total Fat: 18g; Protein: 4g; Total Carbs: 7g; Net Carbs: 4g; Fiber: 3g; Sodium: 154mg; Erythritol Carbs: 4g; Macros: 79% Fat; 8% Protein; 13% Carbs

MADDIE'S FAVORITE CHOCOLATE MALT

Less than 30 Minutes, Dairy-free, Egg-free, Gluten-free, Vegan

SERVES 1 / PREP TIME: 10 MINUTES

When I went to the ice cream parlor as a kid, I had to have a chocolate malt. Well, when I found out gluten had to be removed from my diet, I quickly realized malt was no longer an option. The addition of maca root in this shake creates a delicious malt flavor with no malted milk powder needed. Maddie fell in love with this malt with one sip and it's been her favorite keto treat since.

1⅓ cups unsweetened almond milk

½ small avocado, peeled and pitted (about 2 tablespoons)

1 tablespoon unsweetened cocoa powder

3 to 4 teaspoons powdered monk fruit/erythritol blend sweetener

1 teaspoon maca powder, preferably gelatinized

⅛ teaspoon pink Himalayan salt

3 or 4 ice cubes

In a blender (high speed is best), combine the almond milk, avocado, cocoa powder, sweetener, maca powder, salt, and ice. Blend on high speed for 10 to 20 seconds, or until smooth. Pour in a glass and enjoy.

Variation tip: For a mint chocolate smoothie that tastes just like those chocolate-covered mint cookies you love so much, omit the maca powder and add ½ teaspoon vanilla extract and ¼ teaspoon peppermint extract. Adjust the sweetness level as desired.

Allergen tip: To ensure your malt is dairy-free and vegan, make sure your cocoa powder doesn't contain any dairy products.

Nutrition information per serving: Calories: 260; Total Fat: 20g; Protein: 7g; Total Carbs: 13g; Net Carbs: 3g; Fiber: 10g; Sodium: 301mg; Erythritol Carbs: 12g; Macros: 70% Fat; 11% Protein; 19% Carbs

BANANA PUDDING ICE CREAM

Gluten-free, Vegetarian

SERVES 8 (MAKES 1 QUART ICE CREAM) / PREP TIME: 15 MINUTES /
COOK TIME: 25 MINUTES / CHILL TIME: 12+ HOURS

Banana pudding is the Cowboy's favorite dessert, so it only seems right that I pay respect to this Southern staple by turning it into another favorite treat—ice cream. This keto ice cream couldn't be easier and, thanks to the allulose blend sweetener, the texture is creamy and smooth. Studded with vanilla shortbread throughout, this frozen treat is one for the books! Make sure to use a natural banana extract for the best flavor.

FOR THE ICE CREAM BASE

1¼ cups unsweetened almond milk

1¾ cups heavy (whipping)
cream, divided

¼ cup plus 2 tablespoons allulose
blend sweetener, divided

Pinch kosher salt

5 egg yolks

3 ounces cream cheese,
at room temperature

1 teaspoon vanilla extract

½ teaspoon natural banana extract

FOR THE SHORTBREAD CRUMBLE

4 tablespoons butter,
at room temperature

2 tablespoons monk fruit/erythritol
blend sweetener

1 tablespoon cream cheese,
at room temperature

½ cup almond flour

1½ tablespoons coconut flour

1 teaspoon vanilla extract

TO MAKE THE ICE CREAM BASE

1. In a medium saucepan over medium-low heat, stir together the almond milk, ¾ cup of heavy cream, ¼ cup of sweetener, and salt. Bring to a simmer.

2. In a small bowl and using an electric hand mixer, beat the egg yolks with the remaining 2 tablespoons of sweetener until pale, light, and fluffy. While mixing, slowly stream about half the hot milk mixture into the eggs

(Continued)

(this tempers the eggs so they do not cook). Pour the egg mixture into the pot and cook over medium-low heat for 2 to 3 minutes.

3. Remove the pan from the heat and whisk in the cream cheese, vanilla, and banana extract. Transfer to a container and refrigerate for 2 to 3 hours until cool.

TO MAKE THE SHORTBREAD CRUMBLE

1. Preheat the oven to 325°F.

2. In a medium bowl and using an electric hand mixer, cream the butter, sweetener, and cream cheese until light and fluffy.

3. Add the almond and coconut flours and vanilla. Mix well to combine. Wrap the dough in plastic wrap and refrigerate for 30 minutes to 1 hour, or until firm.

4. Place the dough between two pieces of parchment paper and press it out to about ¼ inch thick. Transfer the dough onto the sheet pan and remove the top piece of parchment.

5. Bake for 10 to 12 minutes until golden brown around the edges and slightly puffed. Remove the sheet pan from the oven and break up the shortbread using a fork to create a crumble. Bake for 3 to 5 minutes, or until golden. Let cool completely on the sheet pan.

TO FINISH THE ICE CREAM

1. Pour the ice cream mixture into the freezer container of an electric ice cream maker and freeze according to the manufacturer's instructions.

2. Once the ice cream is the consistency of soft serve, layer it into a 1-quart freezer-safe container starting with the ice cream and sprinkling some crumble between each layer. Reserve any leftover crumble for garnish.

3. Cover and freeze for at least 8 hours, or until firm.

Troubleshooting tip: A monk fruit/erythritol blend sweetener will not work with this ice cream and will result in a rock-hard texture. I find that the day after this ice cream goes into the freezer, it's completely scoopable right out of the freezer. If needed, let the ice cream sit at room temperature for 5 to 10 minutes before scooping.

Nutrition information per serving: Calories: 355; Total Fat: 35g; Protein: 5g; Total Carbs: 5g; Net Carbs: 3g; Fiber: 2g; Sodium: 177mg; Erythritol Carbs: 12g; Macros: 89% Fat; 6% Protein; 5% Carbs

MEASUREMENT CONVERSIONS

OVEN TEMPERATURES

Fahrenheit	Celsius (approximate)
250°F	120°C
300°F	150°C
325°F	165°C
350°F	180°C
375°F	190°C
400°F	200°C
425°F	220°C
450°F	230°C

VOLUME EQUIVALENTS (LIQUID)

US Standard	US Standard (ounces)	Metric (approximate)
2 tablespoons	1 fl. oz.	30 mL
¼ cup	2 fl. oz.	60 mL
½ cup	4 fl. oz.	120 mL
1 cup	8 fl. oz.	240 mL
1½ cups	12 fl. oz.	355 mL
2 cups or 1 pint	16 fl. oz.	475 mL
4 cups or 1 quart	32 fl. oz.	1 L
1 gallon	128 fl. oz.	4 L

WEIGHT EQUIVALENTS

US Standard	Metric (approximate)
½ ounce	15 g
1 ounce	30 g
2 ounces	60 g
4 ounces	115 g
8 ounces	225 g
12 ounces	340 g
16 ounces or 1 pound	455 g

VOLUME EQUIVALENTS (DRY)

US Standard	Metric (approximate)
⅛ teaspoon	0.5 mL
¼ teaspoon	1 mL
½ teaspoon	2 mL
¾ teaspoon	4 mL
1 teaspoon	5 mL
1 tablespoon	15 mL
¼ cup	59 mL
⅓ cup	79 mL
½ cup	118 mL
⅔ cup	156 mL
¾ cup	177 mL
1 cup	235 mL
2 cups or 1 pint	475 mL
3 cups	700 mL
4 cups or 1 quart	1 L

RESOURCES

Books on the Ketogenic Diet and General Nutrition

The Big Fat Surprise, by Nina Teicholz
The Complete Guide to Fasting, by Jimmy Moore and Jason Fung, MD.
The Complete Ketogenic Diet for Beginners, by Amy Ramos
The Diabetes Code, by Jason Fung, MD
Keto Clarity, by Jimmy Moore and Eric C. Westman, MD
The Keto Cure, by Adam Nally, DO, and Jimmy Moore
Lies My Doctor Told Me, by Ken Berry, MD
The Obesity Code, by Jason Fung, MD
The Salt Fix, by Dr. James DiNicolantonio

Keto Websites & Macro Calculators

The Art and Science of Low Carb: www.artandscienceoflowcarb.com
Burn Fat Not Sugar: www.burnfatnotsugar.com
Cholesterol Code: https://cholesterolcode.com
Diet Doctor: www.dietdoctor.com
Keto Connect: www.ketoconnect.net
Ketogenic.com: www.Ketogenic.com
Livin' La Vida Low Carb: https://livinlavidalowcarb.com
Ruled Me Macro Calculator: www.ruled.me/keto-calculator
Ruled Me: www.ruled.me

INDEX

ACKNOWLEDGMENTS

To my husband and best friend, Chase, thank you for always believing in me, encouraging me on the toughest of days, sleeping with the light on during late-night writing sessions, and never saying anything about the endless piles of dirty dishes on the kitchen counters. To Maddie, my official sous chef, I'm honored that you chose to be my keto partner on this journey; I couldn't have done this without you! To Paige, my official taste tester, I love that you're never afraid to provide brutally honest feedback. You both light up my life. To my mom Sandy, thank you for being the voice of reason on days when I literally couldn't hear myself think and always knowing when I need a good laugh. To Daddy Darrell, your support and love mean the world to me. To my mom Laurie, for showing me how to have fun in the kitchen and introducing me to the delicious world of cheesecake and prime rib.

To my dad, thank you for my pink Barbie kitchen and unknowingly igniting a passion for food and thirst for knowledge that just won't quit. Love y'all!

Also, I'm so grateful for you, my followers and readers. Your support means the world to me!

ABOUT THE AUTHOR

Emilie Bailey is the photographer, owner, and creator of the recipe site *Tales of a Texas Granola Girl*, where she specializes in creating gluten-free, low-carb, and keto comfort food dishes inspired by the Texas and Southern foods she grew up enjoying. After struggling with her weight for more than 20 years, along with complications from polycystic ovary syndrome (PCOS) and idiopathic intracranial hypertension (IIH), she discovered the keto lifestyle and was able to improve her symptoms drastically and, ultimately, her overall health. Today, her PCOS is controlled, her IIH is in remission, and she is passionate about helping others on their journey to better health.

These days, she lives with her husband, the Cowboy, and two girls on a game ranch in Central Texas and also works as the ranch chef. You can find out more about ranch life and browse through more keto recipes at www.TexasGranolaGirl.com.